REVISED SECOND EDITION

JOURNEY OUTSIDE

the

GOLDEN PALACE

DR. CHERYL A. LENTZ

foreword by

DR. TOM WOODRUFF

The Lentz
Leadership
Institute, LLC

Journey Outside The Golden Palace

The Lentz
Leadership
Institute

The Lentz Leadership Institute LLC
9065 Big Plantation Avenue
Las Vegas, NV 89143-5440   USA

Orders@lentzleadership.com
www.lentzleadership.com

The Lentz Leadership Institute books are available at special discounts for bulk purchases for the purpose of sales promotion, seminar attendance, or educational purposes. Special volumes can be created for specific purposes and to organizational specifications. Please contact us for further details.

Revised Second Edition

Library of Congress Control Number: 2010900066

Volume ISBNs
    Soft Cover   978-0-9828740-2-8
    E-book/PDF   978-0-9823036-3-4

    Kindle, Sony eReader, Nook

Cover design by Jacqueline Teng
Design and production by Gary Rosenberg

Printed in the United States of America

10   9   8   7   6   5   4   3   2

Contents

Character is higher than intellect . . .
A great soul will be strong to live,
as well as to think.

—Ralph Waldo Emerson

Foreword

Journey Outside the Golden Palace is a mythical pilgrimage to the hypothetical center of power. Dr. Cheryl takes us on this journey with Henry from The Village of Yore as our guide. On this journey we meet Nada, Earl, and Merlin and learn some of the secrets of the golden palace. Henry's experiences traveling to the golden palace are not unlike the reality we have all encountered in our professional lives.

Dr. Cheryl's rendition of The Golden Palace Theory of Management provides us with a unique perspective on management from the top—down. She creatively describes how the golden palace approach limits the potential success of organizations. By ignoring the talent of individuals outside the palace, who are not ConYesmen, organizations lose valuable sources of innovation and possibility.

Whether or not you are a student of people, leadership, or organizational development you will benefit from reading *Journey Outside the Golden Palace.* The workbook added to this revised second edition promotes practical application of the concepts presented in the book. Enjoy your journey. Invite your friends to come along. See you on the outside!

—Dr. Tom Woodruff

Preface

In writing this book, there was serious consideration given to what I could offer to the vast body of knowledge that already exists 'out there'. I discovered that The Golden Palace Theory of Management (GPTM) was quite simply an idea whose time had come. The purpose of this writing is to give voice to this theory's evolution whose seeds were planted in the late 1980s with my first adventure into the real world of business (translation: first job) upon graduation from the University of Illinois, Urbana-Champaign, IL.

This theory first began with me as its student—a novice with fresh eyes, albeit a bit naïve perhaps, trying to make sense of business *theory* taught in college in order to marry to the *reality of its application* in the 'real' world. My hope is that perhaps you may see your own organizations and experiences within this allegory and the reflections that follow. Perhaps it is now time that the student has learned enough to become the teacher.

I initially expected that immersing one's self in the world of business would allow for great learning adventures. I expected (and secretly hoped for!) the ability to observe and interact with industry experts and mentors with vast repositories of knowledge who would be willing to share their secrets of theory's practical applications. Instead, I remember being intensely disappointed (and sadly remain so for the most part to this day). Time and again I began to realize that this novice college student (me) was able to observe and apply business theory where others quite simply could not. I failed to understand why. Business was not rocket science, at least not to me. Instead, business was elegant in its simplicity, being more an effort of common sense than a result of intense theory or vast experiences.

I remember asking myself often how someone with such lack of experience (me) dare determine or even judge that perhaps I knew more than those with Ivy League or advanced college and graduate degrees with decades of supposed 'real' world experience. Yet few if any were practicing or integrating many business theories or their lessons at all within this 'real' world I had found myself in.

Year after year the disappointment increased. As a result, the Golden Palace Theory of Management was born, created from the result of years of observation, watching industry leaders and managers fail to grasp even the most basic business theory or concept. Slowly GPTM began to evolve, becoming a culmination of now more than 20 years of personal experience as well as the integration of established theory and research—an idea whose time has come, whose stories must be told.

It is my hope that perhaps you might just find that we share similar experiences and observations as we navigate these challenging waters through 'the real world' of business. I hope that you might recognize yourself (or others perhaps?) within these pages and realize that the fundamentals of business are not difficult. By contrast, they are elegantly simple, yet few understand them; fewer still *actually use* them. The secret is to emerge beyond the palace walls of your organization both literally and figuratively and embrace what many in business have simply failed to do.

Part of the reason to publish this book in its second revised edition is to add to these experiences by offering a workbook for discussion, reflection, and refractive thinking, to build upon in Part Two. The purpose of this workbook is to examine each character within the allegory and their subsequent characteristic of leadership more closely—perhaps as mentors or fellow travelers that we may have met along our journey, perhaps even pieces of ourselves that we have created an inner dialogue with—well below the surface.

As our journey progresses and evolves, we can now be offered a chance to work with these specific principles of leadership and perhaps specific personality traits and styles—to find the best fit for us and for the situations we may find ourselves in. Once we have a label, then we feel far more comfortable in knowing what to do with this particularly trait, characteristic, or aspect of leadership—allowing us to expand the depth of our leadership skills and techniques.

Come along with me on this journey. I welcome your company along the way. Perhaps you will share my understanding of the secrets of the Golden Palace. I hope we can share a fellowship, perhaps creating a friend in the business world upon whose vision and direction you can relate. I offer guidance, and above all else hope that all is not lost.

There are indeed solutions. There are indeed answers that can help with whatever situation you may face. You must believe that with every challenge, the seed of its solution is already known; you merely have a journey of discovery ahead to find and unlock their secrets.

Take a leap of faith and follow me. Perhaps one day you will have your own stories to share. I look forward hearing them.

Acknowledgments

Just as the journey for which the Golden Palace evolved was not completed alone, neither were these two books. This second revised edition includes the companion workbook as part of The Lentz Leadership Institute Seminar Series that was created out of necessity. Form does indeed follow function where instead of simply a reiteration of this story, the workbook offers a chance to reflect and work within the lessons and characters within the story that The Golden Palace has to teach us.

My gratitude is extended to Dr. Tom Woodruff for his eloquent words for the foreword, to Jacqueline Teng for her talented pen in designing the cover art for this revision; as well as Gary Rosenberg for updating the book design and structure.

Let me also extend my sincere thanks to the various teachers and mentors along my personal and personal journey for whom made this narrative become a reality. Of particular note, is my doctoral mentor, colleague, and friend, Dr. Elmer Hall whose careful teachings and inspiration continue well beyond the classroom.

JOURNEY OUTSIDE
~ the ~
GOLDEN PALACE

Part
One

CHAPTER 1

Henry the Sage

Once upon a time . . . in a land far, far away, there lived a sage named Henry. A kind and gentle soul, he served as the town philosopher from The Village of Yore. Henry proved to be a man full of bright ideas and strong virtue. He sought to make his hamlet a much better place to live. Henry spent his years working and living among his people, sharing their lives, understanding their wants and needs, and listening intently to their hopes and dreams. These villagers were a common people whose only real desire was to live in a manner they could call their own, and to make comfortable wages while doing something they enjoyed. All who lived there felt a special bond amongst the villagers of Yore, as it was a truly a magical place that cherished its traditions and culture.

Henry found his purpose here, frequently uncovering little ways of improving things. He would tinker with this, and toy with that. People often found him deep in thought pondering his next problem to fix. He increased the local milk supply by helping villager Zelda barter grain and garden items in exchange to import cows from a nearby village so as not to exhaust the current herd. He increased the size of the school by showing workmen how to fix the leak in the roof that had caused a classroom to be abandoned for years through inability and procrastination. The congregation of their church increased merely by reconfiguring the stairs to the entrance so that the elderly had fewer and smaller steps to negotiate.

Henry was a lifesaver to many simply by listening to their needs and cultivating each person to find and implement their own solution; a solution that already existed within the hearts and minds of the villagers. No matter the naysayer, Henry always held a positive attitude and usually found a way to make things better. Sometimes this was simply a matter of implementing ideas that already existed.

Henry's current project was the intent to copy, improve, and implement a new water system that the nearby Village of Progress recently built. The water works had fired his imagination with possibilities. A major breakthrough in moving water had proved far more efficient than the antiquated system in Henry's Village of Yore. The pursuit of having this same water supply system was to be a huge undertaking; one Henry feared that went beyond the simple resources of their village. The approval and possible assistance to create this improved water system would have to come from the very top, the King himself.

Henry had been meeting with the people of his village for years about improving the quality of life in their simple Village of Yore. Each of his fellow villagers offered interesting, pragmatic, and practical ideas and suggestions to share in how they could each contribute to making their lives better. However, the enthusiasm for the new water works proved outstanding beyond measure. They fully backed Henry's proposed project.

For small problems, the villagers, usually with Henry's help, were able to find the solutions themselves. For a new project as large as this however, the ultimate decision-maker had to be the King. Before they could make any changes or improvements, Royal Consent was required.

Inspired by the villagers of Yore and determined to see their mutual dreams of this water project come true; Henry set off to see the King, King William III of Knoddingham.

So when the New Year began, onward Henry proceeded with his plan. Henry sent a messenger and attempted to make an appointment to see the King in the Kingdom of Knoddingham at the Golden Palace. For weeks Henry sent repeated requests via messenger to Johnny, the Royal Assistant from The Village of Knot, in order that Henry might see the King.

Henry patiently sent letter after letter leaving request after request. For 3 months Henry did nothing but wait patiently for a return messenger. At long last, Johnny, the Royal Assistant confirmed that Henry had finally made entry into the Royal Calendar, for the 9th day of the 9th month of the current year.

With that, Henry returned to his village, and packed up his rolls of parchments and plans, filled with all of the information and research, as well as the hopes and dreams, from the villagers of Yore he had gathered over the years. When the time came, off to see King William III Henry went.

CHAPTER 2

The First Day— Nada

On the first day of his journey to see the King, Henry stopped to visit a friend, Nada, the official 'Rearsmooch' from The Village of Not Likely. Henry and Nada talked during lunch about Henry going to see the King. At first Nada listened to Henry politely, as they were old friends from their youth. Nada looked into Henry's eyes and merely shook his head.

"My dear friend," said Nada slowly shaking his head, "I'm afraid your plan is not likely to succeed."

"Why not?" asked Henry.

"Old friend, have you ever *actually met* the King?" queried Nada in a sad tone lowering his voice and his gaze.

"Well, noooooooo" said Henry, purposely elongating the word no as he thought of what next to say. "He is the King, is he not? Surely he cares about the villagers of Yore in his Kingdom?" posed Henry.

Nada thoughtfully looked at Henry for a moment, then slowly and knowingly reached out and patted him on the shoulder. Nada took a moment to reply, choosing his words carefully. "The King is not a very pleasant man, dear Henry. He is considered by some to be very fond of only himself and the Royal Academy of Bean Counters. He is surrounded by the ConYesmen whose only job in the Kingdom of Knoddingham is to knodd their agreement.

The King is the only one amongst them felt to be wise enough to make decisions. He does not listen to others. Unless . . . " With that Nada drifted off for a moment deep in thought, slowly knodding to himself, thoughtfully stroking his chin with his thumb and forefinger. "Yes, that's it!" he cried. Henry sat forward and listened intently.

"You need to **speak** the King's **language**," Nada said excitedly, banging on the table. "Yes, you need to tell him **what's in it for Him.** What will the King get out of this exactly?" mused Nada, somewhat to himself thoughtfully as a slight smile began to form at his lips.

Henry not knowing quite what to say, waited impatiently for Nada to continue.

"Yes, yes. That's it! You must tell the King that by having this new system, The Village of Yore will be able to contribute **more** to the King's coffers and by doing this" snapped Nada, "You will have his complete attention" sitting back on his chair quite pleased with himself, a slow grin forming around his mouth. "Perhaps then, although not likely mind you, perhaps he *might,* just might consider your proposal" said Nada wistfully.

"Y-e-s," began Henry slowly, his eyebrows going up in understanding. "Ah, yes, I think I understand" said Henry. "Money . . . the language of money. Yes I had heard that He and the Royal Academy of Bean Counters were only concerned with counting beans, I mean money," nodded Henry quickly correcting himself in agreement. "Yes, yes" Henry now said with equal excitement, "I do believe you are quite on to something here old friend . . . " smiled Henry.

And with that Nada shook Henry's hand, wished him luck, and Henry continued on his journey.

CHAPTER 3

The Second Day— Earl

On the second day of his journey to see the King, Henry stopped in The Village of That's the Way We've Always Done It to visit a young business man named Earl the Knaïve. He was the youngest businessman in the village who had made an instant fortune as a result of inheriting his father's bakery business. An unusual accident had taken his father's life but a year ago.

Earl the Knaïve had been the envy of all as he simply had been sadly in the right place at the right time. Earl the Knaïve's family had been in the bakery business for nearly the last one hundred years and as luck would have it, a new method had been invented that allowed baked goods to stay fresher longer, allowing delivery to surrounding villages near and far.

Sadly, however, Earl the Knaïve had no business experience, nor any business sense whatsoever. Growing up young Earl had not bothered with learning the family business, preferring to play with his friends instead. Now that he was the only son, the business naturally was bequeathed to him.

Earl the Knaïve awoke every morning and wandered aimlessly through the bakery, giving orders to this one and that, never quite knowing what would work or why. His business continued to make money, so he simply assumed that all was well. He smiled and charmed his way into the hearts of the villagers because of the legend of his dear departed father.

What Earl the Knaïve failed to understand was that his manager Peter Same old-Same old really ran the business exactly as Earl's father and family had done for nearly the last one hundred years. Peter would follow behind Earl the Knaïve and knodd and wink as orders were given. These orders were never followed as workers were told to simply knodd and smile and continue with their work as they always had.

When Henry stopped in at the bakery, Earl the Knaïve had plenty of time to spend with him, having little else to do.

"Hello Earl the Naïve" said Henry, "I am so very sorry to hear of your dear father."

"Thank you Henry" said Earl with a solemn look on his face, "It is good of you to say" pausing to collect his thoughts, "What brings you to our humble village?"

"I am off to see the King" said Henry.

"The King? Whatever for?" queried Earl curiously.

"We are in want of a new water supply system like The Village of Progress. I am hoping the King in all of his benevolence will grant us our desire" said Henry.

Earl looked at Henry in disbelief. "Why would you go to all that trouble? Just use your water supply as you always have and that's that." Earl the Knaïve said confidently with a clip clap of his hands. "Do what I do, I just give the orders, and business just hums merrily along."

"How is the bakery business going?" asked Henry.

"Wonderful. Just great. Good. Well, mostly good" Earl's voice trailed off slightly. "I'm not making as much money as my father used to . . . " Earl admitted slowly, "People must not be eating as much as they used to. It has nothing to do with me of course you understand" Earl said hastily.

Henry asked further, "What seems to be the problem?"

"It must be the manager Peter, Same Old-Same Old. He is getting on in years after all. I'm sure it must be that he just is not as young as he used to be. This is the first time ever we are not as prosperous as we once were . . . " Earl's voice trailed off.

"Nothing to worry about" said Earl cheerfully, regaining his wistful demeanor. "Everything is just fine indeed."

With that, Earl tipped his hat to Henry and with a big grin and a firm handshake, Earl the Knaïve wished Henry well on his journey, putting both hands in his pocket, whistling merrily on his way back to the bakery.

CHAPTER 4

The Third Day— Merlin

On his third day, Henry arrived at The Village of Calm and Clarity to seek out the wisdom of the hamlet's elder, Merlin. Merlin was known throughout the kingdom for his kind heart and his many pearls of wisdom. Merlin was nearly 100 years old, having lived through three wars, and more importantly, three kings of the Kingdom of Knoddingham. Merlin had much experience to share and Henry made a point to seek him out.

Merlin, with his pipe in one hand and his walking stick beside him, was sitting astride the River of Infinite Thought when Henry found him.

Merlin immediately rose upon seeing Henry and offered a respectful hug and kiss on both cheeks.

"Ahh, young Henry. It has been far too long. You were but a wee lad when your father first brought you to me" said Merlin proudly. "You have turned into a fine young man. . . a fine young man indeed. . ." said Merlin more to himself than to Henry trailing off smiling to himself in fond remembrance of Henry and his father's youth.

"Thank you wise Merlin, o' mentor of mine. It has indeed been a long time, has it not? How is the world treating you?" said Henry smiling softly with deep respect for his dear friend.

"Ah . . . the world is but a journey one takes from beginning to end my dear boy. I believe that my journey will one day come to a close and

I will be forever grateful for its many lessons" Merlin said softly, starring off into the River of Infinite Thought with a profound sigh.

"And on what journey are you on dear Henry?" asked Merlin with his eye brows furrowed in deep thought, slowing turning toward Henry.

"I'm off to see the King" said Henry proudly.

"The King? Hmm. *Indeed.*" Merlin puffed on his pipe thoughtfully. "And on what quest are you to see the King?" queried Merlin with raised eyebrows and keen interest.

"The Village of Progress has a new water supply system which I have improved upon and I believe it will help our Village of Yore move forward" said Henry excitedly.

"Hmm. And what have the villagers of The Village of Progress said of this water supply?" asked Merlin.

"They have said great things about how it has increased their ability to carry their goods further and further from their village and has helped them make more money" answered Henry.

"Hmm. And is money what you seek, dear boy?" queried Merlin softly lowering his voice and leaning forward, his gaze intensely focused on Henry.

"Well, uh, yes, I guess" stammering said Henry being caught off guard by his mentor's question.

"Money is but a symptom, a tool, a way of going about one's day. It is not the **what** one does but how one uses their gifts that are of importance dear boy. You would do best to be mindful of this. Money is not happiness; it is not calmness or clarity, or wisdom or knowledge. Money, quite simply . . . just *is*" said Merlin as his gaze trailed off into the river once more, taking a long puff on his pipe.

"*Is?*" queried Henry.

"Yes, *is*. Money is a way for a journey to begin and perhaps to end. It is a tally of one's progress along the way, but not of one's heart, not of one's soul. Money can buy much, but much is not what one will have. Money quite simply *is*. Neither good nor bad, but an instrument of either" Merlin said softly, putting his arm around Henry's shoulder.

"Be careful of what ye seek and the tools one uses to get there my dear boy. And remember, money quite simply . . . *is.*"

And with that Merlin walked Henry to the edge of the River of Infinite Thought and gave him a warm embrace, wishing him every happiness and success along his journey to see the King.

CHAPTER 5

The Golden Palace

When Henry finally reached the Golden Palace, he was awed by its stature and overwhelmed by its immense size and beauty. This was perhaps more than what Henry was prepared for. Shaking a bit at first, he nervously pulled the rope on the Ivory Tower to announce his arrival.

Henry waited and waited outside the palace gate. After what seemed to be hours, Gabbyrial the Gossip, the Golden Palace's Royal Gatekeeper finally answered.

"Who goes there?" the Royal Gatekeeper bellowed.

"It is I, Henry, the humble villager from The Village of Yore who has traveled from afar to see the King" said Henry, nervously pronouncing each word in turn.

"State your business!" commanded the Royal Gatekeeper in a gruff voice, with a bit of annoyance.

"I have an official appointment. I am here to ask King William III to make changes in our village to help us live in a better place" Henry answered meekly, staring down at his feet.

Shaking his head and chuckling at his idealism, the Royal Gatekeeper let Henry pass. "He's in a good mood today. Perhaps he'll see you" chuckled the gatekeeper. "Go up the stairs, around the Ivory Towers, up another set of stairs and you will see there the Royal Assistant, Johnny of The Village of Knot."

So off Henry went to see the King. Henry wandered through the various rooms of the palace; up the stairs, around the Ivory Towers, past the library, around the ballroom, and through the many hallways, up one end and down the other. At last, Henry found the last set of stairs and found Johnny of The Village of Knot, the Royal Assistant. Henry summoned all of the courage he could muster and knocked at the door.

"ENTER!" boomed Johnny, the Royal Assistant in a large resounding voice.

Henry, quivering timidly, walked in to the large room.

"YES?" boomed the Royal Assistant, avoiding eye contact, looking past Henry, visibly annoyed at the interruption.

"I have an appointment in the Royal Calendar. I've waited 6 months and traveled 3 long days to be here. I'm here to see the King" Henry muttered softly.

"Pardon me?"

"I'm here to see the King" Henry stated more loudly with all the confidence he could find in a too loud of voice.

The Royal Assistant slid his glasses down his nose to s-l-o-w-l-y peer over at Henry; looking him up, down, and across for a full 2 minutes. Exhaling with a heavy audible sigh of impatience,

"Yes, and what may the King do for YOU today?" the Royal Assistant finally uttered dripping with disdain, still peering down over his glasses, his head slightly cocked to one side with his eyebrow's furrowed.

"I'm here to discuss important changes we want to make in our village, The Village of Yore" said Henry.

"Oh *you do*? You don't say . . . " harrumphed Johnny, the Royal Assistant from The Village of Knot. "Is His Royal Highness expecting you?" He queried, pausing for effect, already knowing the answer.

"Do you have an appointment?" asked the Royal Assistant rather annoyed and impatiently. "The King is a very busy man you know."

"Umm . . . , uh . . . , yes . . . I . . . , uh . . . , made an appointment to . . . , uh see the King . . . , um. . . 6 months ago" stammered Henry while looking at the floor and shifting nervously from foot to foot. "It was for the the 9th day of the 9th month of the current year of the Royal Calendar" recalled Henry from memory.

Johnny, the Royal Assistant quickly consulted the Royal Calendar and was not able to find Henry's appointment time any where within the Royal Pages.

"No appointment, no meeting!" stated Johnny, the Royal Assistant from The Village of Knot firmly. And with that he slammed the appointment book shut with a loud resounding thump, and went about his business, ignoring Henry completely.

"But wait, you don't understand, I did make an appointment, over 6 months ago. Don't you remember? I made the appointment through you. I left countless messages and waited for 3 months for your reply. You confirmed. Here is the parchment with your signature" said Henry, quite exasperated running out of breath as he pulled the documents from his satchel.

"I've traveled so far, these 3-days and 3-nights, and we have such great ideas. Surely you would honor your word and signature? Certainly His Royal Highness would take pity on me as I am already here? Clearly it is not my fault that your Royal Calendar does not show the meeting. I . . . , I mean we . . ., have so many good ideas to share on improving things" cried Henry out of desperation.

"It does not matter what document has what signature on it. Kno appointment is written in the book" the Royal Assistant said, pointing to the Royal Calendar, "KNO meeting. KNO EXCEPTIONS!" Johnny, of The Village of Knot stated again his voice rising with more force and emphasis, nearly dropping the Royal Calendar in his fury.

Remembering his lunch with his friend Nada from The Village of Not Likely, Henry kept speaking.

"We have so many ways to improve **things**. It could mean more **money** . . . " Henry let his voice purposefully and wistfully trail off, allowing his voice to linger on the word money.

"Things? Money? What kinds of things? How much money?" queried the Royal Assistant, waving his hands about, obviously annoyed, yet curious, not looking at Henry.

"M-o-n-e-y . . . perhaps a great deal of money to add to the Royal Coffers. The improvement of things that will be the King's legacy" said Henry a bit more purposefully elongating the syllables.

Thinking quickly, Henry was able to understand that in order to see the King; he must find a way to convince the Royal Assistant of the value that he and his people could contribute to the King and the Kingdom of Knoddingham, to speak the King's language of m-o-n-e-y.

"Why, yes of course" continued Henry rather smugly, "We have a plan to **t-r-i-p-l-e**," Henry intentionally said, slowly letting each syllable trail off his tongue with affect. "The amount of taxes we would contribute to the Royal Crown, of course."

"Triple, you say?" the Royal Assistant stated, now shifting his full attention to Henry, scratching his chin, obviously impressed. "Hmm, now that just may be something the King would be interested in. *Indeed.*" Johnny said more to himself than to Henry. Perhaps there is a promotion for me, the Royal Assistant thought to himself, faintly amused and growing more pleased. "Wait here," he ordered Henry.

With that, off the Royal Assistant scurried quickly to see the King. Henry was left behind to wait in the huge palace room.

After what seemed endless hours of waiting, the Royal Assistant reappeared, dripping of sweat and apparent fear. Gathering himself together, clearing his throat he boomed in a loud official voice for all to hear (although no one else was in the room).

"Hear ye, Hear ye . . . Announcing Henry, village philosopher of The Village of Yore to see King William III, his Royal Highness of The Kingdom of Knoddingham, and all its lands."

His Royal Assistant then turned with much pomp and circumstance and ceremoniously escorted Henry to see the King.

CHAPTER 6

The King

Henry was amazed at the overwhelming power of palatial room that he found himself in—bigger than all of the buildings in Henry's village, even their town hall. Such ornate offerings, such beautiful tapestries, such opulence as Henry had never before experienced.

King William III was staring out the window, slowly knodding to himself, surveying His kingdom with obvious delight and pleasure, reveling in his power over all he purveyed. After a few minutes and able to return to the present moment, King William III spoke.

"My Royal Assistant says you have traveled from afar to bring me changes you request for your little village, The Village of . . . what was it again? Oh yes, The Village of Yore, that will triple the taxes to the crown. So . . . Speak!"

With that, the King clapped and turned abruptly to leer at Henry with raised eyebrows in much anticipation.

With all the courage Henry could muster, he stammered, "Yes, your Royal Highness I do. (Clearing his throat) "I am from The Village of Yore. We are a good village on the southern edge of your Kingdom sire" lowering his eyes and voice in respect.

"We are quite a ways from the river though. The villagers and I have talked a great deal about how much we could increase the sale of all our village goods if we could only bring the water closer to us. We were hoping that the King, excuse me, your majesty, sire," Henry continued to stammer, visibly shaken "that in your infinite goodness and benevolence would be able to bring the water closer to us. I mean us closer to the water" offering a weak grin.

"We could then work *three* times faster," Henry paused for affect, "and save time by not having to walk to the river each day for water, one hour there and one hour back every day. I have traveled to the nearby Village of Progress to do research and discovered that they have this new system they invented to bring water. I have improved on it . . . and . . ." Henry's voice began to trail off losing his confidence to go on.

The King interrupted, "A new system, you say? I was not aware of any new system," he said more to himself than to Henry, making a mental note to speak to his Royal Assistant immediately.

"The Village of Progress, you say? I'll have to look into this immediately" mused the King as he thoughtfully looked at the window returning to purvey his kingdom, twirling his moustache deep in thought, smirking to himself as he began to quickly tabulate in his head the untold riches that the idea Henry presented before him.

Henry quickly continued "But wait, kind sire, oh benevolent leader, King of the Kingdom of Knoddingham. May I please finish?" bowing for emphasis and respect, attempting to regain the King's full attention and focus.

"The villagers of Progress have increased their revenue by two fold, just in the first 3 months! Surely with that kind of return, we too, I mean The Village of Yore with the added improvements I suggest, could contribute more to the Royal Coffers as well."

"Two fold, did you say? Hmm. In 3 months time, did you say?" The King thought out loud, continuing to mentally calculate his new found wealth. "And then what do you ask of the Crown, my dear boy?" King William III now asked in a new very soft and conniving voice, changing his attitude immediately, now becoming far more welcoming, focusing his full attention on Henry with a tight sneer beginning to form across his lips.

Henry was thinking quickly now, realizing he had the King's full attention, speaking in the Royal Language of money.

"We are a struggling village of only 300 hundred villagers, sire. We do not have enough money to pay for the supplies to build this new system, or the expertise to implement the new system and the added improvements I have invented." Henry stopped for a moment to clear his throat, pausing to give the King time to consider his dilemma.

"Surely, as our benevolent King you see the wisdom of how much more money we could contribute to the Royal Crown's Coffers with such a system? Without doubt, if you could find it in your heart to build this system for us, the village would be a much better and happier place. We would see you as the wise and benevolent man that you are, caring for your kingdom. Your reputation would be heralded throughout the land and known throughout the world . . . " Henry's voice trailed off as he gestured toward the window with a huge arm motion to indicate the lands out the window that the King had been reveling in just a moment before.

"My reputation, did you say? Throughout the land, did you say? Hmm. . ." the King mused to himself while twirling his moustache with a faint smile beginning to curl at his lips, nodding in agreement. "Indeed," muttered the King to himself, "the envy of all the lands . . . "

With two loud claps of his hands—clap, clap—King William III bellowed, "ROYAL ASSISTANT! COME HERE!"

At that, the Royal Assistant, Johnny of The Village of Knot quickly scurried in to the room with his glasses teetering off his nose.

"Yes, sire. You beckoned, sire?" the Royal Assistant quivered back.

"Please gather the Royal ConYesmen for a meeting. Quickly! We have much to discuss" the King announced, with the sneer on his lips curling into a full broad smile. King William III once again turned to focus on the Kingdom of Knoddingham out stretched beneath the window of the Golden Palace, truly deep in thought.

"Yes, sire. Right away your majesty" the Royal Assistant answered as he bowed over and over leaving the room backward in haste.

"And take Henry with you. Our meeting is finished" pronounced King William III. Again, the King loudly clapped twice, signaling that the audience with Henry had ended.

And with that, the King dismissed Henry with a casual wave of his hand. The Royal Assistant, Johnny of The Village of Knot motioned to Henry to follow him and they both quickly left the room, bowing as they exited, never showing their backs to the King as they left the room.

"Well?" demanded the Royal Assistant.

"Well what?" Henry answered, with a puzzled look on his face.

"Well you must have impressed the King with your ideas for him to call a meeting of the Royal ConYesmen" said the Royal Assistant.

"Um . . ., uh, well, I guess I have" stammered Henry finally after much silence and thought, scratching his head, not exactly sure what just happened.

"What happens now?" asked Henry raising his eyebrows in query to the Royal Assistant.

"You wait" said the Royal Assistant firmly without emotion or concern, gesturing with his head, knodding in the direction of the King. "Go back to your Village of Yore and we will be in touch" answered the Royal Assistant curtly with an air of dismissal, a firm head nod, and a casual wave of his hand.

"When will I hear back? What may I tell my fellow villagers?" queried Henry, insistent to know what he could tell the villagers of Yore upon his return.

"Whenever King William III and the Royal ConYesmen have finished of course" impatiently answered the Royal Assistant, ushering Henry to the door.

And with that Henry was led to the hallway with a pat on the shoulder and was quickly dismissed as the door slammed shut behind him with a resounding thud.

"Hmm" thought Henry, "I wonder what happens now?"

Henry thought of this meeting over and over again as he journeyed back to his Village of Yore, replaying every detail in his mind. He had much to reflect upon as he walked over the hills and streams, for the next 3 days, and 3 nights.

Over the next few days, Henry retold of his meeting with the King to the villagers of The Village of Yore over and over, trying to make sense of what happened. No one was quite sure what to make of it, or when they might know more. So many unanswered questions remained. Did King William III really like the idea? Was Henry able to speak the King's language to impress the Royal Academy of Bean Counters as his friend Nada had suggested? When would they know? Would they get their water system? Could they begin to make plans? With winter quickly approaching, much concern hung in the air. . . .

Days, weeks, and months passed without a word from the Royal Palace.

CHAPTER 7

Return to
the Royal Palace

Since Henry's departure, the Royal Assistant, Johnny of The Village of Knot was in a frenzy of activity, making preparations for the big meeting of King William III and the Royal ConYesmen.

On the rising of the sun on the 9th day of the 9th month in the current year, the Royal Count of The Village of White Noise ceremoniously brought the meeting of King William III and the Royal ConYesmen of the Golden Palace to order.

"Hear ye, Hear ye" said the Royal Count with much ceremonial flourish and pomp and circumstance, slowly and with drama.

"Today, in the Kingdom of Knoddingham, under the wise and benevolent leadership of King William III, the meeting of the Royal ConYesmen of the Golden Palace is called to order!" bellowed the Royal Count from The Village of White Knoise, announcing this beginning with a resounding thud of his scepter at the head of the official table for the King William III and the Royal ConYesmen of the Golden Palace.

For 3 days and 3 nights, the King and his 16 men talked about The Kingdom of Knoddingham and all its lands. They spoke of the money paid for this privilege each year to the Royal Coffers by the villagers far and wide as the eye could see. On the 4th day, King William III finally brought Henry's idea up for discussion.

"Hear ye, Hear ye" bellowed King William III. All eyes of the Royal ConYesmen of The Golden Palace were upon him. All 16 of them across the long rectangular table turned their faces to listen, knodding their attention.

"I've had a visitor from The Village of Yore, in The Kingdom of Knoddingham, Henry, the village philosopher" announced the King. The King cleared his throat for emphasis. "Villager Henry asked for a new water supply system to be built that water would be more readily available. He promised that this new system he devised would increase his sales by **two**fold, and his taxes by **three**fold." The King paused for effect, hearing the audible gasp of the 16 Palace ConYessmen as they turned to each other, knodding in earnest.

"Yes, yes? Tell us more, sire" they chorused in unison, knodding their agreement.

"Henry tells me that The Village of Progress is *a-l-r-e-a-d-y* using such a system." The King said slowly and then paused, looking directly at the Royal Count of The Village of White Noise. "Why don't I know about this?" queried King William III turning as he mused out loud, pausing momentarily as he eyed each of the Royal ConYesmen of The Golden Palace in turn.

He continued, obviously satisfied at their discomfort. "They are a tiny village of only 300 people, and cannot pay for such a system" the King chimed, deep in thought, tugging at his moustache.

"Why indeed do I not know about this new water system in The Village of Progress?" King William III mused aloud, again, more to himself than those in the room.

The 16 Palace ConYesmen shuffled in their seats in obvious discomfort, shifting and averting their gaze to the floor.

"Um . . . , I . . . , uh . . . , I mean to say . . . , uh . . . , hmm . . . sire, I'm not quite uh, sure," they stammered one after the other.

"Could we not build this system for The Village of Yore?" said one ConYesmen

"Could we not charge more for this system . . . say four fold?"

"Why not five or six fold?" quipped another.

"We need to find out about this system in The Village of Progress" stated the King. "Yes, *indeed* we must study this. Summon Officious, the Royal Scientist from the Royal Academy of Bean Counters at once!" With that and a regal wave of his hand, the meeting was over and the Royal ConYesmen of The Golden Palace were dismissed.

Days, weeks, and months passed while the water system of The Village of Progress was reviewed and studied in detail by the Royal Scientist and members of the Royal ConYesmen of The Golden Palace.

Finally, King William III issued a proclamation. This proclamation was issued to all the villages of the kingdom far and wide.

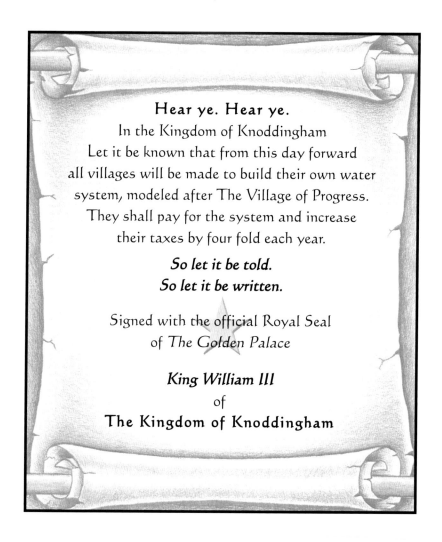

Hear ye. Hear ye.
In the Kingdom of Knoddingham
Let it be known that from this day forward
all villages will be made to build their own water
system, modeled after The Village of Progress.
They shall pay for the system and increase
their taxes by four fold each year.

So let it be told.
So let it be written.

Signed with the official Royal Seal
of *The Golden Palace*

King William III
of
The Kingdom of Knoddingham

Henry read this message that was posted on the entrance to The Village of Yore's Town Hall as was posted in all other villages in The Kingdom of Knoddingham with amazement. He scratched his head in wonder.

"This is not quite what we talked about, now is it?" he mused out loud. "After days, months, and years have passed with no word from The Golden Palace and then this just appears?" Henry sighed out loud, wondering what to do next.

As was customary, there was no challenge or appeal to the crown. Once a proclamation was issued, it was final and to be carried out forthwith.

Henry wondered how he would be able to convince the villagers of the simple Village of Yore that the idea was good and that he had improved their way of life.

What had he truly done?

CHAPTER 8

Journey Outside the Golden Palace Reflections

N arrative stories are often an easy way to communicate the many challenges that we face in order to ascribe meaning and make sense of them, whether in our personal lives, our volunteer work within the community or within the workplace. Story telling offers a way to see ourselves in similar situations sharing similar experiences, offering a learning opportunity disguised as fiction. My goal in presenting this allegory is to offer an opportunity for such personal reflection as I am quite certain each of us can identify with one or more of the characters within these pages. Allow me to be your guide on this journey of self discovery and personal study. Perhaps we will find that we share some old friends.

While reading this allegory you may have discovered that your company lives in a similar Golden Palace. Perhaps your management team makes decisions using the Golden Palace Theory of Management (GPTM) where decisions are made and royal proclamations are issued solely by the King (CEO) and the Royal ConYesmen (Senior Management) with little or no input from the villagers (employees). Does this work for your company? Is this the most effective strategy to employ? This is a personal conclusion that each company and each employee, or stakeholder must come to for themselves. The goal of this allegory is to offer additional guidance and insight that you might consider in your quest going forward.

Each company (and individual) must decide not only what decisions to give voice to, but how the process of decision-making will be carried out. The intent behind this allegory is to perhaps demonstrate how many companies may still function in contemporary society with outdated and archaic methods that for some are no longer useful or effective.

Research offers us guidance when looking at the complexity of organizational decision-making. Often the simplest explanation offers the most insight, wisdom, and guidance.

There is often brilliant elegance in simplicity. The contemporary business elite often believe the answers must be complex, complicated, and in need of intense scrutiny and research by scholars and consultants, members of the Royal Academy of Bean Counters or consultants as it were. Perhaps this simply allegory can offer an alternative.

Countless companies have sought answers and comfort in complex formulas, scholarly theories, and robust equations that many a PhD would struggle to decipher, only to find that often the answers are already in existence. Like Dorothy and her red shoes from *The Wizard of Oz*—she had always possessed the answers within herself. What she lacked was the initial skill to find them, and the self-confidence to believe in them. Organizations behave in very similar ways.

The answers for many organizational decision-making conundrums are not formulas or magic numbers—*external* values if you will. Instead, the answers *are internal* within the brain trust of the collective, where the aggregate wisdom of those, past, present, and future resides in the hearts and souls of the employee, no matter where in the organization the employee or stakeholder may find themselves.

Secrecy outside of the palace walls and purpose of national security is quite frankly dead, trite, cliché, and passé. Meetings behind the walls of the Golden Palace or hiding behind Royal Gatekeepers and ConYesmen (and women) is quite simply outdated and ineffective. There is no need to become entangled within the bureaucracy of the Royal Calendar, or the pomp and circumstance of the Royal Count of White Noise.

All of this activity detracts from the goals of success. The keys to unlocking the secrets of the Golden Palace are transparency and trust, faith in the knowledge of the organization and self-confidence to see it through.

Are there truly any secrets within the Golden Palace, particularly now in the age of technology? The only secret known by Merlin and the River of Infinite Thought is the wisdom that tells us that there are no secrets, only personal decisions to decide what journey one wants to take and what lessons will be heeded along its path.

Walls separate, exclude, divide, and tear down a company at all levels. The Golden Palace symbolizes all of this divisive behavior, an attempt to separate *the Haves* from *the Have Nots,* those within positions of power and influence, and those beyond its reach; The King, and the elitist ConYesmen from the common villagers. This idea of exclusiveness simply moves everyone away from center and the ability to work together.

Again, the question resurfaces; do you or your company live in a Golden Palace? Is there power and privilege only for the select few? Is there power in the secrets that these few *think* they hold either hiding behind their position or title or both? Is the decision-making kept only among the elite, the senior management, those in the C-Suite, the only ones felt to have strategic literacy—the skill, knowledge and expertise in order to most effectively formulate corporate strategy and make strategic decisions (Torset, 2002)? Are no others consulted who are affected in any way? Why are decisions allowed to be made only within the sanctity of the Golden Palace? Are options simply from The Village of Not Likely?

Are those within the palace so insecure of their power and status that they cannot listen to the common villagers? Do the elite only surround themselves with those that knodd their agreement and tell the senior management only what they want to hear? Perhaps senior management only speaks the King's language of money, ceremoniously giving power to The Royal Academy of Bean Counters? Is money the only pursuit as Merlin offered?

Of course, the arguments exist that businesses are in the business of making money, and capitalism is the driving force of our economy. No argument here. It is not the *what* that is of interest to us, but the *how*. As Merlin suggests, money quite simply *is;* a tool, a way of tallying success, neither inherently good or bad, just quite simply *is*. How an organization defines 'is' becomes paramount to their definition of success. How do you want your legacy to be remembered? Perhaps Earl the Knaive, as one who simply wanders through business because of legacy? Perhaps Nada and The Village of Not Likely? Or perhaps Henry with the ideals of believing that people will do simply because it is the right thing to do? The challenge I offer you is not what I believe, but what *is*. And not only what *is,* but what you believe to be for yourself and perhaps your organization.

If the answers you seek are already within your organization and within your people as the Golden Palace Theory of Management suggests, than the only question remains is what will YOU do about it? What legacy will you leave behind? How do you want to be remembered? Do you want to continue to live within the walls of the Golden Palace?

The power of The Golden Palace Theory of Management can be broken with elegant simplicity by merely opening the palace gate to allow your people, your shareholders, most importantly your *stake*holders—everyone that is affected by whatever decision that is in need of being made—to embrace your reality, whatever it may be. Do not assume that the power and the answers lie only behind the throne or within the hands of senior management. True leadership is to be a part of the community of answers; to experience, to involve, to be neither above, nor below, in Merlin's words, to simply *be*. The transparency of leadership is to include *every*one in the Kingdom. Allow the aggregate wisdom within the villagers to be used, included, valued, and respected. No greater power exists than to embrace one's own people, and one's own collective wisdom.

If one can be within the synergy of the moment and the energy of those interested in the success of the company, then the answers will come. It is the journey, where the process becomes the focus, not the individual players themselves. In the words of Merlin, money quite simply *is*.

Give the keys to the Golden Palace to everyone. Then and *only then* will everyone truly be part of the process. There will be no need for the Kingdom of Knoddingham and no need for the ConYesmen (and women). There will be no need for meetings in secrecy behind the palace walls to decide the fate of those not present. There will be no need for Royal Pronouncements from the King that especially fall short of the mark if the mark, if even in the discussion at all. There is no land of Knot, and no Village of Not Likely, instead only possibilities to seek what is already known by those already there both past and present.

The wheel is already here, already invented for all to see—no need to reinvent what your people already know. No need to confine oneself to the Royal Academy of Bean Counters and count beans. The journey begins with asking the right questions, not in search of only the *perceived* right answers. There may be many right answers, many inputs, much collective wisdom, and knowledge that can coexist in harmony. It is possible that many are correct in their perception, from their vantage point and their voices deserve to be heard.

Do you possess the strength to be willing to take a leap of faith to find the path to get there? Or do you still believe in fairytales?

Leadership comes in many forms, and sometimes it comes softly. One sincere moment can change the world, one—little 'w' or our little corner of the world at a time. When lots of little 'w's combine, the ripple affect can ultimately change the world by default, 'the big W.'

Answers exist. We simply need the leadership of transparency to trust enough to let go and work with others to find them. Trust your people; trust them to perhaps fail at first in order to succeed. As leaders, we merely have to create the environment to succeed by opening the Golden Palace to let the light in. Only then will solutions truly be possible.

Good luck in your journey. I'll be here waiting to share your stories and your ultimate successes. Go forth and conquer as the world is in desperate need of leaders like you . . .

JOURNEY OUTSIDE
~ the ~
# GOLDEN PALACE

Part
Two

THE LENTZ LEADERSHIP INSTITUTE
EDUCATIONAL SEMINAR SERIES

The Golden Palace
Theory of Management

Companion Workbook

CHAPTER 1

Introduction
The Companion Workbook

Part One of this book was a journey that was more than 20 years in the making—a marvelous example of the process to which this journey outside of the Golden Palace refers. It grew out of my very first job out of college. At the time, I was quite concerned with my expectations—not realizing that these might have been out of place. I expected that everyone would know more than me, either as a result of their study in college, experience, trips around the sun, or a combination thereof.

What I began to discover is that I would have to learn to manage these expectations and begin to see learning as grand opportunities in perhaps how *not* to do things—at least at first. I remember initially being profoundly disappointed that I was not learning very much in the 'real' world for which I had accepted membership. What I *was* learning was disappointing at best, as I only seemed to be learning how *not* to do things *first*, particularly within the worlds of management and leadership. This often begged the question—when would the good 'stuff' start?

Since the human condition is about story telling—this is my story about the genesis of the Golden Palace Theory of Management (GPTM) and why it is so important. The technique chosen to tell this allegory is a story using fictitious characters set back in the 'jolly ole days of

England'. Why? The purpose is to protect the identities of those that I have met along the way.

Through the main character Henry, the story has its tour guide—the lens through which the metaphors of people and beliefs are seen. How we learn to view these characters is a result of how we choose to view the world through this tour guide. How accurate is Henry in what he sees? The magic of this story is in the transformation that Henry experiences along his journey—potentially mirroring the one each of us face.

Bolman and Deal (1991) offer the concept of using frames in which to view the world in which to bring perspective into focus. "Frames are both windows on the world and lenses that bring the world into focus. Frames filter out some things while allowing others to pass through easily. Frames help us to order experience and decide what action to take" (p. 11). Many of these characters within Part One of this book are people all of us have met and perhaps worked with along our own personal journeys. This book is meant not to poke fun or embarrass anyone in particular per se. Instead, the wisdom offered within these pages is meant to offer personal stories of people and behaviors, specifically with how one chooses to manage and lead. These personal stories are mirrors perhaps of what we each have experienced, personal stories we each can find connection with and guidance from.

I discovered early for example that many people in positions of leadership, particularly at the apex of the organization, seem to concern themselves solely with the concept of power and their personal reputation, not necessarily what may be the best possible outcome for everyone within the sphere of influence these leaders serve. This is where the Golden Palace Theory of Management has its genesis.

Only those in senior leadership positions within the executive office or C-Suite were felt to understand and employ the concept of strategic literacy in order to possess the skill, knowledge, and expertise in order to most effectively formulate corporate strategy and make strategic decisions (Torset, 2002). As a result, for a particular organization in which I began my career, the senior management team would often go off site for their yearly strategic meeting at some undisclosed location to 'create' the long terms plans for the coming years in increments of 1, 3, 5, and 10 years.

What I found strangely interesting and often faintly amusing is that when they returned from this secret location, they offered their results as if they were royal pronouncements coming from Moses himself. The peasants (translation: employees in the company) would be given the benefits of their wisdom and thinking, yet having not been a part of the process in any way. Herein lays the problem. This Senior Management Team did all the critical thinking, and went through the entire strategic decision-making process *without* having all the answers, and *without* involving many of the people that did.

Pech and Durden (2004) argued that "many organizations fail because of weaknesses in the decision processes of their leaders" (p. 66). And Pound continued this logic arguing that "most performance crises are not because of incompetence or wayward managers, but because of failure in judgment" (Crossan, Fry, & Killing, 2005, p. 121). The conclusion that this leads to is simply that there is something inherently wrong with this process of decision-making within the boundaries of this Golden Palace. Why would one make a decision without *at least attempting* where possible to involve all of the appropriate people with all of the appropriate knowledge?

My doctoral dissertation focused on this strategic decision-making process and participative styles of involving those in the organization beyond those in senior management. After 20 years of my personal journey in quest for answers and my doctoral research, the book was finally put to paper in an attempt to tell my story as seen through the eyes of my fictional character and conceptual guide, Henry.

The purpose of this book is to advance learning via the story telling technique of the allegory—providing both reflection and entertainment as one begins to see the world through Henry's eyes. In my personal travels, I have not seen anything like the GPTM 'out there' so I remain confident that this will offer value to the wider body of knowledge, providing another way to look at the workplace and the strategic decisions that are made within its walls.

Part of what is new to this revised second edition, is this addition of Part Two—the companion workbook—containing the ability to reflect upon these specific characters more in-depth with their intertwining stories and life lessons they share with us. The intent is to offer guided and focused critical thinking and personal reflection upon various relevant and applicable topics of leadership as found through the experiences of these characters. The quest is to "ask and ponder the rights questions, to dare to think differently . . . ultimately to lead where others may follow or to risk forging a new path entirely" (*The Refractive Thinker*™: *Volume I*, 2009, back cover).

The companion workbook begins entrance into The Lentz Leadership Institute's Educational Seminar Series to work through each topic at a pace appropriate to the reader for a more in-depth personal reflection using each character as one's own personal guide and mirror.

Safe travels as this journey begins . . .I look forward to hearing your stories.

CHAPTER 2

Henry the Sage
The Village of Yore

O ften there is an idea for which the time has simply come. *The Golden Palace Theory of Management,* in my humble opinion is one such idea. Its genesis is quite simple, yet its culmination has taken more than 20 years to emerge and crystallize. Let's begin this journey and meet our main character, Henry, the sage from The Village of Yore.

This *idea* of Henry—as a guide through this metaphor in his quest to find knowledge—started to come together early in my career, during my first job as a college graduate. Quite simply, when I began my journey into the real world of business as it were, I had expectations for those in positions of influence above me that they would know more than me. This seems to be quite simple and logical, being a realistic expectation particularly from the vantage point of a young college graduate trying to make her place in the world. I had not yet really experienced life or the work force of any real consequence quite yet. I expected mentors and guides to emerge to build upon what I had *begun* to learn as *theory* in my collegiate years.

In all candor, I was quite disappointed in my early discoveries, and that is how this theory of The Golden Palace began to evolve. Henry's character embodies this naiveté—always believing in the people of his Village of Yore and The Kingdom of Knoddingham, and of course its beloved bureaucrats (The Royal Academy of Bean Counters) and its rulers (King William III) and all those in positions of corporate governance and power as within the fictious realm of The Golden Palace.

I found that many people within this Golden Palace felt it necessary to manage from a position of weakness. They felt the need to hoard and manipulate power and knowledge as if to maintain their place in the world and their organizations—to demonstrate and justify their need to be employed.

Many people seemed to follow this formula as if there was some unwritten rule I had yet to learn that to be an effective manager or leader, one had to rule in secret, within the shroud of palace walls, protected by palace guards and gatekeepers, ensconced in layers upon layers of distance and secrecy between leaders and the people they served. The more important one believed themselves to be, the more layers surrounded them, and the more distance and challenge it would take to reach them as if these various layers were considered the very symbols of their power themselves. This began to beg the fundamental question of how many assistants and layers did one truly need? These layers were not necessarily layers of success but boundaries *to* success, and potential signs of weak character and fear.

And so it is that we meet our beloved Henry, the main fictitious character (fictiously named to protect the innocent or perhaps the ignorant or guilty of those I have met along my 20 year journey). Henry emerges in our story as a humble sage from The Village of Yore that has evolved as a result of these collegiate and organizational experiences. Through the eyes of Henry, he becomes both tour guide and teacher. Through his interactions with the metaphors of people and beliefs that exist on many levels within these pages, he exists to provide discussion between many management and leadership philosophies, demonstrating that many are quite ineffective and outdated.

Many of these characters are people all of us have met and worked with along our personal and professional life's journey. The use of allegory is meant not to poke fun or embarrass anyone in particular (since it is set in a completely different time frame with intentionally chosen fictional names). Instead, this story is meant to offer personal stories of people and behaviors, specifically with how one views and interacts with the world.

Those that are senior stewards of the company [insert your company name here] do **all** the strategic thinking and make all the strategic decisions, without necessarily having all the answers, or involving the people that do. Within this story, King William III will act as the Chief Executive Officer (CEO); and the royal palace and all its bureaucrats will act as the senior stewards of The Kingdom of Knoddingham [insert your company name here] who take over this critical thinking process for Henry. As Henry seeks their needed approval, he finds himself confused and bemused as the system literally takes over the process of a seemingly simple decision—transcending its simplicity and need to the corrupted principles of money, power, ego, and greed.

Because of this perceived power, some consider this lack of knowledge as a sign of weakness. If one should walk out of one's office and cross the great divide—the Golden Palace that separates management or senior leadership from the rest of the staff (peasants) to ask questions or to involve outside of the safety of the palace walls, one might as well cross into the great abyss.

Note how King William III simply makes decisions with the primary focus of money, not intent or purpose for either specific villages or the overall kingdom. Instead of fulfilling Henry's need for his village to serve the villagers, King William III sees his duty as the sole source of power and wisdom—to think for Henry—all in terms of the bottom line. This sustains the glory of money without involving those that would be affected by the decision.

Yet, this collective repository of wisdom is exactly what was needed. The Village of Progress did indeed have the knowledge and the needed answers—all accomplished without the knowledge or consent of The King—and could have been easily involved with providing their aggregate wisdom and expertise, not only as subject matter experts, but as needed experts in the very the process itself.

How interesting that the King was not even aware of the *progress* of The Village of Progress. Perhaps this situation is simply a reflection of the bureaucracy where it seems it is simply easier to beg forgiveness than ask permission? How sad is this philosophy with the potential to keep all of these secrets within its village boundaries, not offering this learning for the ultimate greater good of the entire kingdom and beyond its palace walls.

Let us return to dear Henry, a peasant himself, and a recognized leader within this humble village, The Village of Yore. Henry recognized the need to benefit from the wisdom of everyone in the village who were willing to offer an idea, or their own pearl of wisdom, often more than one. Henry realized early that his was not the task in which to *have* all the answers, merely to be the collective host or guide to lead others to *find* the answers and how to be a champion of change—a change agent (*The Refractive Thinker*™: *Volume III: Change Management*, 2009).

He found a willing audience where all he had to do was to ask. The answers he found were in abundance. There were no walls, no distance between the villagers; just a common goal in which to exchange ideas and learned wisdom to better all their lives, embracing the varied talents of the villagers themselves.

After attentive and careful listening to the villagers, Henry became their organizer, their spokesperson, their champion, their leader who was willing to take their quest to the next step, the higher authority for approval, the King, King William III, of Knoddingham. This is often the position that a leader finds themselves in, merely having the willingness to serve, to practice servant leadership, to take the initiative and simply begin. A leader is someone to whom others look to with confidence and trust—a safe keeper of the message and vision, with the desire to change the world or at the very least their corner of the world.

Leadership is not always a function of talent or knowledge, simply a desire and passion to believe in the dreams of one's self and others. Learning will come along the way. One simply needs to put one foot in front of the other—and have the courage to begin. In the immortal words of Ralph Waldo Emerson—"Do not go where the path may lead, Go instead where there is no path, and leave a trail" (Emerson, 1803-1882).

Henry does not shy away from the duties of the mantle of leadership. Instead he relishes the opportunity, setting off on a 3-day journey to see King William III to champion the cause of the villagers of Yore—to embrace the desire to be an agent of change—to make a difference.

Along the way, Henry meets several guides: Nada, the official 'Rearsmooch' from The Village of Not Likely; Earl the Knaive, from The Village of That's the Way We've Always Done it; and Merlin, from The Village of Calm and Clarity. In the coming chapters, each will focus in detail on the meanings of these various characters and the villages from which they come—where the goal is to see what lessons that they have to share with Henry and how we each may benefit in return.

SEMINAR SERIES WORKSHEET

Servant Leadership

The servant leader practices leadership that transcends the self to truly and only serve the needs of others.

Robert K. Greenleaf coined the phrase 'Servant Leadership' in his essay *The Servant as Leader,* first published in 1970. In that essay, he said:

> "The servant-leader is servant first . . . It begins with the natural feeling that one wants to serve, to serve *first.*" (Greenleaf, 1970, para. 1).

1. What does servant leadership mean to you?

   _____

   _____

   _____

2. How did Henry practice this kind of leadership?

   _____

   _____

   _____

3. How do you practice this kind of leadership?

   a. In the work place? _____

   _____

   b. In the home? _____

   _____

   c. In the community? _____

   _____

4. What is the value of this type of leadership?
   What are the benefits?

_____

_____

_____

5. What is a leader's top priority when practicing this?

_____

_____

_____

6. What was Henry's top priority and focus?

_____

_____

_____

7. Is leadership beyond one's self interest truly possible?

_____

_____

_____

8. What actions can we specifically take to practice this?

_____

_____

_____

9. How can servant leadership change the world?
   What can you do to further this aim?

_____

_____

_____

CHAPTER 3

Nada—'Rearsmooch'
The Village of Not Likely

In Chapter 2, *Henry* embarked on the first day of his 3-day adventure to see King William III, the King of Knoddingham. Henry's quest was in search of approval for the plans for a new water system for The Village of Yore.

On his first day, Henry stops to see his friend, *Nada,* the official 'Rearsmooch' from The Village of Not Likely. How many of us know someone of Nada's stature and name, one who seems to be in a perpetual state of agreement? Perhaps the old adage: *'He who does not stand for something, will fall for anything'* applies here. The character Nada represents these types of people; they go wherever the wind may blow them, or their boss—lacking direction, conviction, or individual thought. They are the result of focusing on the opinions of others to be in agreement, particularly with those above them, never venturing too far on their own.

We have all met or worked with this person at least once along our personal journey, always with an angle; always trying to work a deal that always seems to work in their favor. This someone always seems to be a parrot—seeming to exist merely to reaffirm whatever the prevailing opinion and focus of group wisdom may be of others in positions of power or influence above them. Hmm. What a *coinkydink.*

Nada represents ideals that have met the harsh realities of life and corporate behavior—hitting them head on. This is where one learns compromise and how to blend in to not make waves, simply nodding in agreement to those in positions of power or influence, personifying the opinion of others—demonstrating little or no original thought or conviction. Is there a person beneath this surface one may ask?

For some of us, at certain times in our lives it may be more appropriate to be a follower, instead of a leader. And that is perfectly acceptable. Much research confirms that to be a good leader, one must perfect the art of followership first.

Sometimes we may simply prefer to follow or perhaps even *need* to follow, to ensure that we might achieve our goals and those of the organization and communities we serve. Sometimes, though, this idea of followership simply takes a wrong turn, taking a very different path than followership may have intended, with a very Machiavellian 'the ends justify the means' type of philosophy instead. For some, it is not often noticed that there is anything wrong with this type of following—until we have compromised ourselves too much that we no longer know where we end, and another begins. This is not what followership intends, to blindly follow in the path of another to only gain favor, at the expense of self.

The concept of Nada tries to convince us of the honorableness of this quest to serve ourselves through serving others, believing that it is not possible to get what we want without using such alternatives. Life has taught some of us that without these alternatives, perfecting them as nearly their own art form–we would forever remain a member of The Village of Not Likely, a victim of our own beliefs, and perhaps even our own success. The lesson that is taught (or perhaps the lesson that is learned?) is that we must manipulate the situation to obtain what we want or perhaps even what we feel entitled to have or perceived we've earned.

Nada has learned the fine art of not only extreme followership, but what may be ideally and often affectionately known as 'kissing up' or 'brown nosing' certainly stretching the intent of followership which was not meant to manipulate those above where one learns to speak the language of one's audience, specifically of those in positions of power or influence, to gain promotion or favor, with a 'what's in it for me' kind of attitude. Followership was not intended to manipulate those above to curry favor or promise. Instead followership was intended to learn to follow first from those that know how to lead.

The concept of Nada *chose* to learn the art of what some consider skillful negotiation and manipulation—what some consider the clever art of *managing from below* (Maxwell, 2005). Nada offers this idea to Henry that to get what **Henry** needs for The Village of Yore, Henry has to begin thinking as if **he** were the King, translating this to a *what's in it for me* mentality, to determine and highlight what benefits the King would receive from this 'arrangement' **as well as** Henry. By creating this *impression* that everyone wins, particularly preserving King William III's self-interest, the outcome is assuredly a victory. *Or is it? What will our intrepid hero decide?*

By appealing to the King's vanity, sense of greed, and need for power, Henry *could* choose to frame his proposal in the King's best interest as Nada suggests. To achieve the needed outcome, Henry could heighten this sense of persuasion and appeal to this idea of being self-centric and *could* learn to speak the King's language, specifically the language of money.

Since, King William III is focused solely on how to enrich the bottom line, Henry could use the tools at the King's disposal, specifically the perception in the belief of the power of money that is contained within the purview of The Royal Academy of Bean Counters. This appeal to *what's in it for the King* kind of altruism could be a very effective technique indeed.

Henry could learn to use this powerful technique, using the King's own self motivation in support of a more outcome based thinking approach. This then begs the question, is this appropriate? Fair? Effective? Ethical? And to whom? Nada is suggesting a wee bit of a ruse in contrast to simple directness, and business negotiation. Is this professionally appropriate and ethically adequate? Does this embrace being emotionally and socially intelligent?

How many of us learn to profit from taking advantage of the needs and wants of our bosses, supervisors, and friends; those in positions of power and influence, standing between us and our goals? By *appearing outwardly* benevolent **as if** our *one and only* true purpose is the altruistic goals of another, we *appear* to be seen as caring, compassionate, and sincerely interested in the benefits to others.

Come now. Is this *really* true? Are we being intellectually honest? *Really?* Does it matter if our intentions are honorable, or merely the outcome or results of favorable persuasion and skillful manipulation? Perhaps you may offer that if everyone gets what they want or need, where is the harm, right? Utilitarianism suggests after all that this is considered ethical behavior if the greatest benefit is achieved for the most people. Is it not a win-win for all concerned? Does intent matter if the outcome and consequences are favorable? To whom? And at what cost? Again—this begs the question—does it really matter? To some the process matters very much indeed.

Perhaps we might want to look through this lens or concept of emotional and social intelligence as well—the idea of carefully planned and executed social calculation and purposeful dynamics—where "the picture enlarges beyond a one-person psychology—those capacities an individual has within—to a two person psychology: what transpires as we connect (to others)" (Goleman, 2006, p. 5). Our reputation could begin to tarnish and establish itself as one who comprises, *ever so slightly at first,* with only the most benevolent of goals and purposes; that they of course take great care to assure us and remind us, time and time again. Over time, however, these little compromises and altruistic justifications begin to erode one's sense of self and perspective becoming a crisis of character, a cross roads of ethics and morality—where we must look to "be intelligent about our social world" (Goleman, p. 11).

Where is this nexus of where our goals end and another's begin? How does one "take the measure of a relationship in terms of a person's impact on us and ours on them"? (Goleman, 2006, p. 12). Have we allowed ourselves to fall victim to the curse of being a forever member of The Village of Not Likely and this is our sole path to succeed? Do we lack the social skills to be intellectually honest with regard to our behaviors as well as our intentions?

Goleman (2006) refers to this as *empathic accuracy*

which represents some argue, *the* essential expertise (that) is social intelligence . . . (where) this ability distinguishes the most tactful advisors, the most diplomatic officials, the most effective negotiators, the most electable politicians, the most productive salespersons, the most successful teachers, and the most insightful therapists. (pp. 88–89)

How can we balance our personal philosophy with the need for such essential expertise of social intelligence?

What may one anticipate as the end result? Are we happy with who we are *or* who we have *chosen to be?* Have we honestly taken the time to think or reflect on the possibility? For some of us, we have to consider the possibility that we may very well be less than altruistic and more myopic and self-centric than we had hoped. Do we *really* put the needs of others ahead of our own yet still get what we want or need—or is this simply what we tell ourselves so we can sleep at night?

Who we are is the legacy to which we leave our mark on the world. Are we then satisfied with the outward effects and appearances of these gifts? Is Machiavelli correct in that unless we control our destiny and use whatever means necessary, we would not otherwise succeed? Would our ideal hero Henry find comfort in the use of such transparent techniques? More importantly would you?

SEMINAR SERIES WORKSHEET

Emotional and Social Intelligence

The emotionally and socially intelligent leader practices leadership that understands interpersonal dynamics as well as social dynamics to make sense of people. The purpose is to explore self satisfaction with personal relationships and a sense of self and purpose in life.

Daniel Goleman (2001) coined the terms: *emotional intelligence* and then *social intelligence* to explore emerging sciences with vast implications to explain social dynamics.

1. What does emotional intelligence mean to you?

   _____

   _____

   _____

2. What does social intelligence mean to you?

   _____

   _____

   _____

3. How do you practice these aspects of leadership?

   a. In the work place? _____

   _____

   b. In the home? _____

   _____

   c. In the community? _____

   _____

4. What is the value of this type of leadership?
   What are the benefits?

   _____

   _____

   _____

5. What is a leader's top priority when practicing this?

   _____

   _____

   _____

6. What was Henry's top priority and focus?

   _____

   _____

   _____

7. Is leadership beyond one's self interest truly possible?

   _____

   _____

   _____

8. What actions can we specifically take to practice this?

   _____

   _____

   _____

9. How can emotional and social intelligence change the world?
   What can you do to further this aim?

   _____

   _____

   _____

CHAPTER 4

Earl: The Knaive

The Village of That's the Way We've Always Done It

On his second day, Henry stopped to see his friend, *Earl the Knaive* (pronounced: naïve) from The Village of That's the Way We've Always Done it. Earl and Henry had been chums from their youth, and Henry stopped along the way to pay his respects as Earl's Father had unexpectedly passed away in the last year. As customs dictated with Earl being the eldest son, the bakery business of his father was automatically bequeathed to him. While no experience, Earl was quite frankly—at the right place at the right time—and the right gender as in the time of jolly ole England. Or was he?

If one looks at the big picture, was Earl really serving others as a result of this place in the family? Is ignorance truly bliss? Earl wandered aimlessly through life and subsequently through the bakery business, getting by, as the saying goes on the kindness of strangers and perhaps on his good looks and charm.

The real force behind Earl was the bakery's manager, Peter, *Same old-Same Old*. With a nod and a wink, Peter dutifully followed Earl as they made the daily rounds at the bakery. Whatever Earl would say or to whomever he would say it, Peter would simply give a knowing glance, an understanding nod, a wink here, and a smile there. This created an unwritten rule that Earl's commands were not necessarily to be followed.

The bakery and Peter had established a reputation for following in the footsteps of Earl's father and the already established patterns of The Village of That's the Way We've Always Done It. Earl did not have the trust of his staff, as they knew he did not have a keen business sense. Earl just did not understand the Bakery Business or any business for that matter. Just because he had the good fortune, dare we say good timing, to be a man during these days of old where it was simply automatic that the business should fall to him as the eldest son—business sense or not. The unfortunate reality was that the business was not doing as well as it had in the past.

The truly sad commentary here is that Earl lived up to his nickname of being naïve and simply did not understand what was going on around him. As the proverbial ostrich in the sand, Earl simply went through life, smiling happily, blissfully unaware that the sky was quite literally falling around him. He only knew of one way, to purposefully and blindly perpetuate the past.

Earl could not see that anything was broken; therefore there was no need, or any incentive to fix this brokenness. There was no need for new thinking, creative thinking, or purposeful or forward thinking, critical thinking, or refractive thinking. Earl simply was a manager believing that his duty was to maintain the status quo of today using the techniques of the past. He did not understand that time did not stand still—and neither could he. Change happened. Life happened. Yet Earl did little or nothing, save to smile and tip his hat and contently wish you a good day.

When Henry stopped by, Earl was pleasant, the picture of good health, believing he held a prosperous business. Earl could not understand why Henry had such a need and sense of urgency to change the world. Earl liked his world just the way it was—thank you very much. Earl found comfort and peace in the way it had been since his father, and his father's father before him.

Earl could not fathom that times could or would change. He could not envision the speed at which technology would change or that upgrades to the business might be needed some day with the advent of new processes, new inventions, or discoveries. Earl could not under-stand why anyone would want to *intentionally* change or bother for any reason whatsoever. Why expend the effort? If everything was going smoothly, Earl simply thought that everything was quite fine indeed. After all, if Earl could not see it, then of course Earl would not have to respond nor feel the need to do anything about it. Steward leadership was not part of his character.

Ignorance was the foundational element to the balance in this vil-lage—he and equally as important those around him—were content to simply travel along the path they had always been on. What direction they should take was of no interest or concern. Life simply would move merrily along. Earl did not think he or anyone else in this village would need to be a leader, as he was content with the life of a manager whose day to day activities were quite frankly the same as Earl had been told as of the days of yore.

While Henry was in pursuit of improvement, efficiency, and progress, *Earl the Knaive* was content to stay within the safety and confines of this idyllic comfort zone, just wandering merrily and happily along. Despite that business was not booming, and certainly not at the level of profit as during the days of yore and his father and his father before him, Earl did not equate this change in leadership—namely him—with the lack of profit or business prosper. Instead, Earl believed that none of this was certainly *his* fault, instead laying the blame at the foot of his manager, Peter, *Sameold-Sameold* and other anomalies to which Earl separated himself for any accountability, correlation, or causality. After all, he really did not do anything at all. *And* Earl liked it that way.

How many of us live in Earl's world—simply content with the same activities day in and day out? We deplore change, we avoid newness, we ignore conflict, and we simply put our heads in the collective sand and only do what is required of us at the very minimum, and sometimes not even that. What has happened to us, the excitement we once held to change the world as Henry would like to? Have we lost our drive? Our willingness to explore new challenges? Have we been left behind, intentionally and blissfully unaware of the world around us? Perhaps it is safer this way, our ability to remain purposely and blissfully ignorant and unaware?

Perhaps we have been caught up in the culture of our workplace where we are surrounded by our own version of Earl and Peter: wonderful men, who are pleasant, jovial, and happy, yet completely complacent, apathetic, naïve' and quite content with both the inner and outer worlds of The Village of That's The Way We've Always Done It. Could it be that we, like them, prefer our world to be safe and predictable staying firmly rooted within our comfort zones?

There are those amongst us who prefer not to see how we are responsible or accountable for much of anything. After all, *really*, we are just here to do our jobs, show up, and collect a paycheck, right? What can *we* really do anyway? Have we as a culture and society really given up? Perhaps instead given *in?* Do we live within this fragile façade because we actively choose to or simply allow the choice to be made for us? Either way, we simply tip our hats, give a jolly ole smile with a nod and a wink, and saunter on our merry little way down the same road we oft have found need to travel. If we have no destination in mind, then any road will do. After all, we like things just the way they are—gentle lady, kind sir—thank you very much. Good day.

What advice might Henry offer Earl? What advice would you offer? Would this advice even make any difference to either Earl, Peter, or anyone within this surreal and unrealistic world? Perhaps it is simply safer to allow those to exist in the splendor of ignorance? How many days can this splendor truly last–particularly within the business speed of contemporary times? Can we truly afford to live within this village?

SEMINAR SERIES WORKSHEET

Steward Leadership

The concept of steward leadership is an employee-focused form of leadership. This aspect of leadership focuses on that which empowers followers to make decisions and have control over their world.

The emphasis for this leadership style is upon the characteristics of kindness and patience, being respectful and humble, offering honesty and firm adherence to commitment. This includes the:

- Stewardship of people
- Stewardship of products and services
- Stewardship of the community
- Stewardship of the environment
- Stewardship of the Social Fabric. (Smith, 2004, para. 18–22)

1. What does steward leadership mean to you?

   _____

   _____

   _____

2. How could Earl benefit from this form of leadership?

   _____

   _____

   _____

3. What kind of decision-making does Earl practice? Is it effective?

   _____

   _____

   _____

4. What would change for The Village of That's The Way We've Always Done It with this type of leadership?

_____

_____

_____

5. How did Henry practice this kind of leadership?

_____

_____

_____

6. How do you practice these aspects of steward leadership?

   a. In the work place? _____

   _____

   b. In the home? _____

   _____

   c. In the community? _____

   _____

7. Is leadership beyond one's self interest truly possible?

_____

_____

8. What actions can we specifically take to practice this?

_____

_____

9. How can steward leadership change the world?
    What can you do to further this aim?

_____

_____

_____

CHAPTER 5

Merlin—Day 3
The Village of Calm and Clarity

On his third day, Henry arrived at The Village of Calm and Clarity to seek the wisdom of the hamlet's elder, Merlin. Merlin offers us one of the most complex characters of the story?—the one who talks to Henry in specific metaphors, content with asking the right questions as a seeker of the right answers. Merlin becomes the mentor—the wise voice within us that evolves as the result of time, experience, and the ability to reflect and cultivate life's lessons. Merlin had much experience to share and Henry was wise enough at this point in our story, and in his life, to visit him as part of his journey.

Merlin, with his pipe in one hand, and his walking stick beside him, was sitting astride the River of Infinite Thought when Henry came upon him. Merlin often spent his days deep in reflective thought, gazing into this river that changed ever so slightly as the sands of time calmly traversed its banks. This was a calming respite of solace spent adjourned with nature returning to its fundamentals for guidance. As Merlin had learned, moments spent in reflective thought—dare I say refractive thought as well—were an investment of the heart, and an investment of character where time taken rewarded rich dividends.

Life was too hurried as evidenced through the words and personality of the concept of Merlin. The *answers* to life's never ending challenges were never discovered amidst the frenzy of day-to-day living. Instead the pursuit of the right *questions* was to be found in the disci-

....

plined focus of peace and calmness, uninterrupted moments in harmony with nature. Time spent amongst this river bed was indeed the most pleasured filled moments of comfort that Merlin had found throughout the years, offering simpleness and clarity that is often overlooked in the hurried pace of contemporary times.

How often do we take the time to calm this outward chaos so that we may cultivate inner peace? How many of us look within ourselves in search of answers? How many of us trust our inner voices in which to hear the wisdom that already exists within? How many of us take time to focus on our own vision and mission statement to create the picture on the top of the Jigsaw Puzzle Box top?

It was within this purposeful silence for which Henry was in search of its lessons. "The world is but a journey one takes from beginning to end dear boy" mused Merlin—contemplating the finiteness of life itself—the hurried pace at which we proceed, missing so much along the way. Merlin had expected that one day Henry would indeed find himself on a journey such as this for which clarity would be needed. Merlin was pleased that this time had come.

As Merlin and Henry continue their conversation, Henry slowly arrived at the topic at hand and told Merlin that he was off to see King William III—to curry favor from the King to grant his Village of Yore the much needed new water supply. *When the student is ready, so the teacher will come,* thought Merlin with an approvingly smile and nod.

How many of us have mentors that are waiting for us? As with Dorothy in *The Wizard of Oz,* our mentors realize that certain parts of the journey must be made alone—intentionally allowing our struggles so that we alone may determine the outcome to find the answers we seek. When we alone are ready, conversations such as those Henry sought out with Merlin, his mentor will come.

Throughout their conversation, Merlin looks to the River of Infinite Thought, always pausing thoughtfully to touch his faithful companion—his walking stick. Merlin's purpose was to be a thoughtful listener, a sounding board for Henry in which to deepen his personal journey.

Merlin becomes a guide—directing Henry to places where he should look, offering questions he might consider, ideas he must contemplate, paths he might consider to travel.

By lowering his voice, Merlin captures Henry's attention, pondering the specific concept of money. This question is what catches Henry off guard, wondering what it truly may imply; captivated by the potential new path that Merlin may be blazing for which Henry may choose to follow.

The conversation continues as Merlin offers additional pearls of wisdom for contemplation. Merlin offers his thoughts with regard to the concept of money. Not to confuse effort with outcome, Merlin offers that money is but a tool, where judgment is passed on what one does with one's tools—explaining the journey from the *what* to the importance of *how*.

Henry stared into the River of Infinite Thought as well, not yet grasping the full meaning of these words that Merlin offered. Henry did not yet understand that money was a judgment word; a word without meaning until given one, by the participant, the holder, the lender, the owner, the context that ascribes some meaning to it. Money is not inherently good, nor bad.

Money quite frankly is an inanimate object, neither human nor being, neither with the ability to think nor feel. Yet money is invariably the subject and focus of much discussion and repartee. What is the fascination exactly with this coin or paper on which the many faces from history appear? Money and surely the *concept* of currency in the broadest sense of the word have been around since the beginning of time. Money is a tool, a function of measure, a metric of trade, a way of contemplating the world as one may perceive it to be. Money, quite frankly in the words of Merlin *just is*.

With those words, the exchange between Merlin and Henry ended. Henry went on his way still deep in thought regarding what his mentor was trying to teach him. Merlin was oft a master at metaphors and lessons masked in riddles and questions that only the recipient in time after careful thought would be able to answer.

How many of us have been given advice along our own personal journeys only to find its wisdom several days, years, or even decades later as the pieces began to fall in place as understanding finally offered sense and meaning? At the nexus of experience and wisdom is where true learning can take place—our 'aha' moments of self reflection and discovery. Our personal epiphanies often come in life's quietest moments—once the 'noise of life' has softened as our own River of Life and Infinite Thought gurgles merrily forward. Perhaps only then are we given the most precious gift of all—the gift of ourselves and the choice of our future.

What will Henry make of these gifts that Merlin and the River of Infinite Thought offer? Will the river give up its lessons to be master and friend to Henry as it has served Merlin throughout his many trips around the sun? How does this latest puzzle piece fit within the lessons that Henry has begun to discovery throughout this 3-day journey? How might this change Henry's strategy in which to see the King?

How many of us still remain at the banks of the River of Infinite Thought—still trying to unwrap the mysteries of its ebb and flow—to make sense of the big moments in our lives? What if we were given the vision to know what course to travel, what path to take? How might our journey then change?

SEMINAR SERIES WORKSHEET

Leadership:
The Jigsaw Puzzle Principle

Kouzes and Posner (1987) suggested that:

> It is easier to put the puzzle together if you can see what is on the box cover.
>
> In any organization, people have different pieces of the organizational puzzle. Members may have detailed descriptions of their roles and responsibilities, but very often they lack information about the 'big picture'—about the overall purpose or vision of the organization. (pp. 98–99)

1. What does The Jigsaw Puzzle Principle mean to you?

   _____

   _____

   _____

2. How did Henry practice this kind of leadership?

   _____

   _____

   _____

3. How do you practice these aspects of leadership?

   a. In the work place? _____

   _____

   b. In the home? _____

   _____

   c. In the community? _____

   _____

4. What is the value of this type of leadership?
   What are the benefits?

   _____

   _____

   _____

   _____

5. What is a leader's top priority when practicing this?

   _____

   _____

   _____

6. What was Henry's top priority and focus? Merlin's?

   _____

   _____

   _____

7. What actions can we specifically take to practice this?

   _____

   _____

   _____

8. How can having vision change the world?
   What can you do to further this aim?

   _____

   _____

   _____

   _____

CHAPTER 6

The Golden Palace
The Royal Gatekeeper

The gatekeeper—a wonderful concept and metaphor that appears in one's personal life as well as the corporate landscape. To whom do we trust within our inner circle to guard the castle's inner keep? What purpose does this gatekeeper serve exactly? For some this gatekeeper is the first level of bureaucracy—intended to offer a level of security and judgment by another—to keep out those that are deemed unworthy. The gatekeeper has the ear of those in power, however also retaining power of position in their very existence as well. This person decides to whom to grant favor, and to whom to allow passing into their master's inner circle. For those wanting to approval, a gatekeeper can be a formidable ally or a very difficult conquest indeed.

Conventional wisdom offers that if one is trying to curry favor with a new client, often currying favor with their personal gatekeeper first is the strategy one will employ. Perhaps the first tactic is to focus on a personal assistant, a lower level management title, even a lackey in some parlance—whatever the title, one must pass this test—this boundary and broker this power abyss before one can move on—to gain an audience with 'the King' or for whomever the gatekeeper is in their employ.

Are we the gatekeeper for someone above us in our organization? For a community leader? Our spouse? Perhaps even our children? What criteria or yardstick have we constructed to keep these people 'safe from the outside world', whether mere peasants or more serious bureaucrats? To whom do we allow to intrude upon our solace and privacy? To whom do we allow to be our filter to the world—the eyes and ears in which to judge if thou might pass?

Why is there this perceived need to protect others in this way? Why does one need an intermediary level between one's self and others beyond their walls of their own personal and perhaps organizational golden palace? Does this simple function imply power? Importance? Or is it something deeper than this, perhaps protecting our self confidence, our self esteem, our ego—our perceived values of ourselves and others?

This idea of power comes in two forms, either positional power or personal power (Bass, 1990). The idea of the power of one's position is our focus here. By the concept of the very title and concept of the gate-keeper, regardless of one's actual title, one controls access to the person to which one guards the gate. Johnny, The Royal Assistant from The Village of Knot is the character that represents this concept—guarding to preserve the inner sanctum of the King.

We all know someone like Johnny, both the bureaucracy and the figurehead to whom he is slave to. Henry waited months and months to garner favor of an appointment through Johnny, only to appear in person where there is no official recording of the meeting in the official Royal Calendar.

It is intentionally not revealed whether or not this recording of the appointment was intentional or not. Perhaps it could have been a mere oversight—a typical bureaucratic snafu or clerical error. Or perhaps was there something more afoot? How many of us have wondered at our attempts to see the King (read: CEO or someone higher than we are in the organization to which we report) and whether or not we were intentionally thwarted, intentionally avoided? These gatekeepers were skillful in the art of manipulation and avoidance *until* there became a shift in power.

When Johnny, The Royal Assistant is persuaded by Henry that perhaps it would be in Johnny's best interest, then—and only then—does

Johnny take a genuine interest. When Johnny ever so casually mentions that this meeting could add money to the Royal Coffers—now Henry has the Royal Assistant's complete attention. We have returned to our previous time spent with Nada's and his advice of speaking the language of one's audience to get their attention, and to offer them an argument of *what's in it for them* to garner their help wherein then does the gate open to which the gatekeeper controls.

This appeal to greed and ego is what finally triggers the release of the palace walls where Henry is given passage. When Johnny believes it is in his best interest and then of course that of the King believing that perhaps the King would reward Johnny for allowing this person to meet the criteria and pass through these imaginary gates held firmly in place by The Golden Palace and its keeper of the key.

This challenges the very boundaries of benevolence and altruism. Are we truly testing the boundaries of power only when it is in the best interest of ourselves to do so? Or is there a true function to this gatekeeper in which the best interest of the one beyond the gate is preserved? Machiavelli again would beg the question as to does it matter? If the means justifies the ends (i.e. Henry was able to get to see the King and it benefitted all parties)—did this process and hence this power brokerage process really matter?

The ideal is referent power, where one complies simply because one identifies with or admires with the person who is in the position of power to gain the person's approval. Is this not the goal, to gain the approval of another as a sign of respect and validation, as opposed to a *what's in it for me* mentality, preserving ego and greed? What does Henry do? More importantly what would *you* do?

SEMINAR SERIES WORKSHEET

Positional Power and Referent Power

Bass (1990) defines positional power as "power that is inherent in the formal position occupied by the incumbent" (p. 920).

Yukl (2006) defines referent power as "the target person complies because he/she admires or identifies with the agent and wants to gain the agent's approval" (p. 166).

1. What does the concept of power mean to you?

   _____

   _____

   _____

2. How did Johnny the Royal Assistant practice this kind of leadership? Henry?

   _____

   _____

   _____

3. How do you use these concepts of power in terms of leadership?

   a. In the work place? _____

   _____

   b. In the home? _____

   _____

   c. In the community? _____

   _____

4. What is the value of this type of leadership?
   What are the benefits? What are the dangers?

_____

_____

_____

_____

5. What is a leader's top priority when using these kinds of power?

_____

_____

_____

6. What was Johnny's top priority and focus? Henry's? The King?

_____

_____

_____

7. What actions can we specifically take to use power effectively?

_____

_____

_____

8. How can the use of power change the world?
   What can you do to further this aim?

_____

_____

_____

CHAPTER 7

King William III
The Kingdom of Knoddingham

The idea of coercive power is certainly not something new. Coercive power seems to be the most common power that many of us have had the most experience. We however must take great care to consider that there is a definite difference between leadership as influence and leadership as power.

In this case, King William III uses not only his power of his position, his ability to reward and withhold rewards from those within his kingdom; he also holds the ability to influence. House (1984) defined power as "equated with the capacity to produce effects on others'. These effects are achieved by the exercise of authority, expertise, political influence, and charisma . . . each having a different base or source and each having different effects" (as cited in Bass, 1990, p. 226). Henry faces the King having nearly all elements of the affects of power as described here.

The authority of King William III stands between Henry and the reaching of his goal. Only the King within the Kingdom of Knoddingham has the authority in which to grant the permission to both build the water supply as well as open the Royal Checkbook in which to pay for its construction.

The question for Henry is how to potentially find a way to navigate these turbulent waters in which to present an argument to the King to persuade the King of the advantages of this request. As reminded by his visit to Nada from The Village of Not Likely, Henry reviews the advice he was given—to speak the King's language—the language of money, to persuade the King to use his power to grant this request.

Henry decides that based on Nada's advice where the King is solely concerned about the King; Henry has to appeal to this greed and vanity to use this power brokerage to produce the desired effect. So Henry goes right for the bottom line, driving his point home to show why it is in the best interest of the King to grant this request. Henry also softens this request to couch this bottom line driven by money to show how the outcome of this request would increase the King's reputation—showing how the outcome alone would ensure that the peasants would think of the King on only benevolent terms—based on the affects and outcome of the decision. By stroking the King's ego in this way, he could appeal to all areas of the King's leadership persona, his power base, his appeal to personal vanity, and traits of character or lack thereof. One then observes that leadership can then be coerced as the exercise of powerful followers who understand the dynamics of the power brokerage relationship.

As asked in previous chapters, does it become a concern of how? Machiavellian doctrine assumes that only the outcome is of importance—in this case the use of power—for an effective outcome. Henry potentially gets this new water supply for The Village of Yore and the King gets two to four times the additional monies to the Royal Coffers—all in the name of royal benevolence to his followers. Everyone wins, yes?

Perhaps not. Power is not the same as influence. Power does not have the same outcome as leadership where leadership is defined in the broadest sense of the word as the ability to influence another. "We need to separate the holding of power because of one's person, one's office, the willingness to exercise it, and the tendency to actually do so. Studies tend to confuse all four and sometimes even fail to distinguish between power and influence" (Bass, 1990, p. 226).

As a result, *why* and *how* are very important to the outcome. It is intentionally that the King is painted as a vainglorious person whose only concern is with himself and money. Riches are the language that the King speaks. Instead of simply appealing to doing the right thing—

to help the villagers improve themselves, instead it becomes a function of having things done right—in this case in the interests of the King.

Sadly each one of us is often faced with having to make this choice—between doing things right (managers) or doing the right thing (leaders) (Bennis & Nanus, 1997). This is often a source of frustration as many of us live in the ideal plane where we do not believe we should have to choose no more than Henry. Henry has to choose to potentially compromise his ethics in such a way as to have to manipulate the situation in which to appeal to the King's character and traits to get the desired outcome. Henry would have far preferred as most of us would—to simply ask the question for the content of the request to be of importance. Henry is not asking for himself, and the villagers are not making an unreasonable request to better themselves and their village and the kingdom by default.

Yet, Henry is wise to see that in Merlin's words, money quite simply is—neither positive nor negative—simply a function of context. In this context, Henry has to appear to be what he is not—to manipulate and pander to the needs of the King and the Royal Bean Counters by default to show them why it is in the King's and their best interest to do so. While there are many more positives to consider, the only ones that are of interest to the King are his need to assuage his desire for greed as part of his power, and his ability to lie to his ego—assuring that his decision is truly based on benevolence and altruism.

The challenge that each of us face is what will we do when faced with such a situation? Will we simply present our request to the King (CEO) and his senior leadership (Royal Academy of Bean Counters and the Royal Scientist) or will we choose to compromise our ideals and principles in order to speak the King's language of money and greed that we may have the desired outcome regardless of the efforts needed to get there? Only each of us will have to decide how we wish our reputations to be regarded. Is this really a big compromise, a hill in which we will choose to die on? Or do we simply tell ourselves that if the outcome is favorable and everyone gets what they want—wherein lies the true harm? I will leave to each of us to decide . . .

SEMINAR SERIES WORKSHEET

Leadership:
As Power or Influence?

In the broadest sense, leadership may simply be seen as the ability to influence one other person (Daft, 2008).

> We need to separate the holding of power because of one's person, one's office, the willingness to exercise it, and the tendency to actually do so. Studies tend to confuse all four and sometimes even fail to distinguish between power and influence. (Bass, 1990, p. 226)

1. What does the concept of power mean to you?

   _____

   _____

   _____

2. How did Johnny the Royal Assistant practice this kind of leadership? Henry? King William III?

   _____

   _____

   _____

3. How do you use these concepts of power in terms of leadership?

   a. In the work place? _____

   _____

   b. In the home? _____

   _____

   c. In the community? _____

   _____

4. What is the value of this type of leadership?
   What are the benefits? What are the dangers?

   _____

   _____

   _____

   _____

5. What is a leader's top priority when using these kinds of power?

   _____

   _____

   _____

6. What was Johnny's top priority and focus? Henry's? The King's?

   _____

   _____

   _____

7. What actions can we specifically take to use power effectively?

   _____

   _____

   _____

8. How can the use of power change the world?

   _____

   _____

   _____

9. What can you do to further this aim?

   _____

   _____

   _____

CHAPTER 8

The Royal Pronouncement
The Secrets of the Golden Palace

Managing expectations is often a cornerstone of leadership principles. How does one balance what one expects vs. what actually happens? Henry struggled with trying to understand the process of King William III and his various Royal Bureaucrats as his request for The Village of Progress's water supply was considered.

While Henry had not yet been through this process and therefore did not know officially what would happen, he did have an expectation that he and his request would be handled with respect and consideration, to be judged on its merits and its outcome. Henry did not understand nor feel comfortable with the fact that he was not part of the process. With a quick wave of a hand, Henry was simply dismissed by Johnny, the Royal Assistant, without any indication of what might happen.

Days, weeks, and months passed without a word from the Golden Palace about Henry's request. How often have our requests met with such silence and distance? Many of us are not concerned with the answer itself, so long as we are given the courtesy of receiving one. We simply want to have our time respected and to be considered worthy of at least a timely response to our reasonable request.

In the absence of information, we often are left to our own devices and thought processes to wonder at the outcome and the very process itself. The longer the time frame, the more doubt creeps into our psyche. Did we perhaps miss something? Could we have done a better job? Could we have offered different arguments, perhaps ones that were more salient? Was it us personally?

We are simply in search of answers and it appears to be reasonable to expect them. It is reasonable to expect that if we have taken the time and effort to make the request of someone that they would at least have the courtesy to respond in some way. Even if the answer is no, simply taking the time to respond to our request, our email, our telephone call would seem to be the respectful way to proceed.

Instead, without any contact or warning, Henry receives the same communication that everyone in The Kingdom of Knoddingham does—the Royal Pronouncement that simply appears out of nowhere one day on the wall of their village Town Hall. Henry is left to wonder. It was not exactly what was discussed in the initial meeting, was it? Henry was left wondering what to do. He had his villagers, his constituents, his followers to whom he had risen to the challenge to champion their quest. What *would* he tell them? What *could* he? What *should* he?

Henry was expecting that he would be contacted by the King or the Royal Palace or someone to at least let him know what was going on—to keep him in the proverbial loop. At the very least he expected to be the first to know of the decision, not simply to be part of the peasants en masse when the Royal Pronouncement was made, not only in his village, but throughout The Kingdom of Knoddingham.

Does this not speak volumes regarding the true motivation behind Henry's request where it was not Henry or his villagers or even the idea that was presented that was of importance? Instead, it was as Henry had suspected, the outcome, the addition to Royal Coffers that was of main importance. If these offerings were so good from The Village of Progress, and then to include Henry's request from The Village of Yore, the King and the Royal Bureaucrats simply expanded to include the entire kingdom, after all if 1 is good, 10 is better right?

How is it that Henry was not involved in the decision-making process itself, let alone informed of its outcome? After all he was the one initiating the request, would it not be at least *reasonable* to expect a response, something for which he could offer his followers first? Is it not the importance of the process and the outcome as well as the participants of value?

Since there was no challenge to the crown (CEO or senior leadership) Henry was left to scratch his head in wonder, not even able to ask further questions of clarity or confirmation. How many Senior Leadership Teams behave this way? They simply take some junior level staffer's request or idea and run with it, dismissing them out of hand. Those in these upper level positions give little credence to the person or persons generating the idea, believing all are of no importance or value. There is no heed paid to morale or employee well-being. Is there no consideration or respect given to those for whom have taken the time to present this idea and its potential? Should they not be involved in the process? Or at the very least given advance notice of the decision?

Often those in senior leadership forget the effect on the masses. They see only the benefits to the bottom line. They miss the indirect affects, the effects on the value of the peasants in their kingdom, the effect on their person, their morale, their character.

Hiding behind the confines of The Golden Palace is no way to lead a company. One cannot simply forget the ideas of the workers, the value of those that carry out the orders of those in power. One cannot simply be stuck in Machiavellian times with only seeing the end result. The effects of process—the effects of the strategic making process *is* the importance. It is not in finding the right solutions; it is in asking the right questions for which the right solutions emerge. The Golden Palace Theory of Management is the very antithesis to the participative decision-making process.

According to Pech and Durden (2004), "many organizations fail because of weaknesses in the decision processes of their leaders" (p. 66). It is the process of which garners the importance to one's organization—the ability to involve those who are the stakeholders—those who are affected and have a stake in the decision. Crossan, Fry, and Killing

(2005) believe that "most performance crises are not because of incompetence or wayward managers, but because of a failure of judgment" (p. 121) believing that strategy thinking is needed throughout the organization, not simply from those *and only those* at the top.

This transformation of the strategic decision-making process is what has emerged shifting the paradigm from authoritarian leadership to collaborative leadership. This concept of inclusiveness, put forth by Floyd and Wooldridge (1997, 2000) years ago has emerged into the age of the knowledge worker where *all* knowledge is important and of strategic value to the organizations' leadership (Holt, Self, Thal, & Lo, 2003; Peters, 2005; Raelin, 2004).

The question becomes on what processes do your organizations use? How do you include people beyond the walls of those in the Golden Palace? How do you respond to the requests of employees within your kingdom?

SEMINAR SERIES WORKSHEET

Inclusive Leadership: Participative Strategic Decision-Making

The concept of inclusiveness, put forth by Floyd and Wooldridge (1997, 2000) years ago has emerged into the age of the knowledge worker where *all* knowledge is important and of strategic value to the organizations' leadership (Holt, Self, Thal, & Lo, 2003; Peters, 2005; Raelin, 2004).

Involvement of employees wherever they appear in the organization should be included in the strategic decision-making process to include this knowledge regardless of where the knowledge comes from or who possesses it, in order for the organization to sustain competitive advantage within the global marketplace.

Research demonstrates that an effective strategic decision-making process that embraces this inclusiveness of all relevant employees is an important feature to the subsequent success of the strategic process of the organization and is lacking within many of today's organizational leadership structures (Floyd & Wooldridge, 1997).

1. What does the concept of inclusive leadership mean to you?

_____

_____

_____

2. How did Henry practice this kind of leadership? The King? The Royal Bureaucrats?

_____

_____

_____

3. How do you practice this type of leadership?

   a. In the work place? _____

   _____

   b. In the home? _____

   _____

   c. In the community? _____

   _____

4. What is the value of this type of leadership? What are the benefits?

   _____

   _____

   _____

5. What is a leader's top priority when practicing this?

   _____

   _____

6. What was Henry's top priority and focus? The King's?

   _____

   _____

   _____

7. What actions can we specifically take to practice this?

   _____

   _____

8. How can inclusive leadership change the world?
   What can you do to further this aim?

   _____

   _____

CONCLUSION

Beyond the Palace Walls

As we find ourselves at the end of our journey, our goal is to spend time in reflection to review our purpose to our journey outside the walls of the Golden Palace, to tear down the boundaries that separate and divide. Instead of distance and bureaucracy, our goal is to pursue transparency and true leadership that comes from true internal character and inclusiveness.

What have we then learned through these travels as seen through the eyes of our tour guide, dear Henry? What do the rest of characters of the Golden Palace have to offer us in terms of the overall lessons and concept of leadership? What are our stories?

Our dear Henry is the constant thread that weaves our tapestry together existing on many levels of both storyteller and personal guide. He offers us a gentle reminder that a leader does not necessarily have to be the smartest person in the room or the person at the top of the organization. Instead a leader merely has to have a desire to lead, a desire to serve those for whom the leader has chosen to champion their cause. A leader merely has to have the courage to begin.

Henry then becomes more than a mere tour guide, but a mirror, a reflection of ourselves, who we are at this particular time in our life, as well as an outgrowth of the people we have met along the way and the choices we may have made. Henry then offers us the chance to see other reflections of parts of ourselves, Nada 'the rear smooch', Earl the Knaive, culminating in a chance to meet ourselves face to face at the River of Infinite Thought with Merlin—an elder version of ourselves—the older, the wiser, the one who has taken this journey and emerged with its lessons in which to guide those that follow. Knowing what we know now if we would have only known then, however we were unwilling or unknowing or simply had not yet arrived at that place in our journey quite yet.

Henry begins to learn patience with bureaucrats, learning to accept that power and influence are not the same. Henry learns humility and the ability to make decisions about his legacy and for what he wants to be remembered. Does he want to be remembered for the character of outcome as well as intent? Does he want to be remembered for having to learn to speak the language of another to curry favor? Is the outcome what is important, or the process in how one gets there?

How does Henry mirror these lessons? Does it matter that he gained an audience with the King merely because of what Henry could do for the King—promising riches and untold fame and wealth?

How is Henry treated through the process? Only as important as the benefit he brings to others? How does Henry react to the confusion? It is interesting to note the fact that he is not the first one told of the outcome, as he simply finds out with everyone else as part of the Royal Pronouncement. Is Henry the victor or simply the victim?

Perhaps what may be needed is to begin anew yet again at this current time in our career to create—a blank slate—an empty canvas for which we can begin to ponder the gifts that life offers us, in this case through the lens and reflective mirror of Henry. Perhaps instead of settling for what we see, instead of settling for merely thinking outside the box, we challenge what the world reflects back to us, refractively challenging and questioning its lessons to perhaps begin by building an entirely new box, beyond boundaries and precedence. What will the River of Infinite Thought whisper to us amidst its quiet and reflective shores? Were these lessons different at different points along our journey? Were we receptive of its lessons and wisdom? Will we be receptive to its lessons in the future as our journey continues? Will we quiet our minds and the noise of our lives enough to listen?

What are the many lessons of The Golden Palace? Are Henry and his cast of characters finished teaching us? What new characters may we meet as the journey continues?

Take a walk outside of your company's Golden Palace, dare to journey behind what you may find there. Dare to live beyond the boundaries. Dare to think differently, behave differently, expect differently. Dare to live.

References

Bass, B. (1990). *Handbook of leadership: Theory, research and managerial applications* (3rd ed.). New York: NY. The Free Press.

Bennis, W., & Nanus, B. (1997). *Leaders: Strategies for taking charge* (2nd ed.). New York: NY. HarperBusiness.

Bolman, L. G., & Deal, T. E. (1991). *Reframing organizations: Artistry, choice, and leadership.* San Francisco, CA: Jossey-Bass Publishers.

Crossan, M. M., Fry, J. N., & Killing, J.P. (2005). *Strategic analysis and action* (6th ed.). Toronto: Prentice-Hall.

Daft, R. L. (2008). *The leadership experience* (4th ed.). United States: Thomas South-Western.

Holt, D., Self, D., Thal, A., & Lo, S.W. (2003). Facilitating organizational change: A test of leadership strategies. *Leadership & Organization Development Journal, 24*(5/6), 262. Retrieved June 26, 2005, from ProQuest database.

Floyd S., & Wooldridge, B. (2000). *Building strategy from the middle: Reconceptualizing strategy process.* Thousand Oaks: Sage Publications Inc.

Floyd, S., & Wooldridge, B. (1997, May). Middle management's strategic influence and organizational performance. *Journal of Management Studies,* 34(3), 465. Retrieved March 3, 2005, from ProQuest database.

Goleman, D. (2006). *Social intelligence: The new science of human relationships.* New York, NY: Bantam Books.

Greenleaf, R. (1970). *What is servant leadership?* Retrieved December 27, 2009, from www.greenleaf.org/whatissl/

Kouzes, J. M., & Posner, B. Z. (1987). *The leadership challenge: How to get extraordinary things done in organizations.* San Francisco, CA: Jossey-Bass Publishers.

Lentz, C. (2007, May). Strategic decision-making in organizational performance: A quantitative study of employee inclusivessness. *Dissertation Abstracts International, AAT: 3277192.* (UMI No. 3277192).

Lentz, C. (Ed.). (2009). *The Refractive Thinker* (Vols 1–3). Las Vegas, NV: The Lentz Leadership Institute.

Maxwell, J. (2005). *The 360° leader.* Nashville: TN: Nelson Business Publishers.

Pech, R., & Durden, G. (2004). Where the decision makers went wrong: From capitalism to cannibalism. *Corporate Governance,* 4(1), 65. Retrieved October 1, 2005, from ProQuest database.

Peters, T. (2005). *Leadership.* New York: DK Publishing Inc.

Raelin, J. (2004, Jan/Feb). The "bottom line" of leaderful practice. *Ivey Business Journal Online,* 1. Retrieved June 26, 2005, from ProQuest database.

Smith, M. (2004). Steward leadership in the public sector. *Global Virtue Ethics Review,* 5(3), 120. Retrieved on June 29, 2009, from ProQuest Database.

Torset, C. (2002, July). 18th Egos Colloquium. *Strategic literacy: The great question.* Retrieved October 8, 2005, from www.dauphine.fr/crepa/ArticleCahier-Recherche/Articles/ChristopheTorset/ChT-EGOS2002%20.pdf

Yukl, G. (2006). *Leadership in organizations* (6th ed.). Upper Saddle River: NJ: Pearson Education.

About the Author

Southern Nevadan author Dr. Cheryl Lentz holds several nationally accredited degrees; a Bachelor of Arts (BA) from the University of Illinois, Urbana-Champaign; a Master of Science in International Relations (MSIR) from Troy University; and a Doctorate of Management (DM) in Organizational Leadership from the University of Phoenix School of Advanced Studies.

Dr. Cheryl, affectionately known as "Doc C" to her students, is a university professor on faculty with Colorado State University-Global, and the University of Phoenix.

Dr. Cheryl is a proud and active alumnus of Alpha Sigma Alpha Sorority.

Additional published works:

Strategic Decision Making in Organizational Performance: a Quantitative Study of Employee Inclusiveness.

The Refractive Thinker™: An Anthology of Higher Learning, Chapter 10: Fail Faster, Succeed Sooner.

The Refractive Thinker™: Volume II: Research Management: Chapter 3: The Modified Ask-the-Experts Delphi Method: The Conundrum of Human Resource Experts on Management Participation

The Refractive Thinker™: Volume III: Change Management: Chapter 10: Strategic Change Management: The Importance of Inclusiveness.

Index

Other Books by the Lentz Leadership Institute

The Refractive Thinker™: Volume I: An Anthology of Higher Learning

The Refractive Thinker™: Volume II: Research Methodology

The Refractive Thinker™: Volume III: Change Management

Coming in the Spring of 2010

The Refractive Thinker™: Volume IV: Leadership Ethics

The Refractive Thinker™: Volume V: Globalization

MasterMinds: Graduate Anthology: Abstracts & Essays

*Available in e-book, Kindle, and individual e-chapters by author

---

Telephone orders: Call us at 877 298-5172

Fax Orders: Fax form to 877 298-5172.

Email Orders: orders@lentzleadership.com

Speaker Bookings: speakingengagements@lentzleadership.com

Website orders: Please order online via the website: http:www.lentzleadership.com. PayPal™ accepted.

Postal Orders: The Lentz Leadership Institute LLC
c/o Dr. Cheryl Lentz
9065 Big Plantation Avenue
Las Vegas, NV 89143-5440   USA

The Lentz
Leadership
Institute LLC

Please send the following books:

❏ *The Refractive Thinker™: Volume I:*
  An Anthology of Higher Learning

❏ *The Refractive Thinker™: Volume II:*
  Research Methodology

❏ *The Refractive Thinker™: Volume III:*
  Change Management

Paperback: $18.95 plus applicable tax and shipping.
E-books: $12.95 plus applicable tax.
Individual e-chapters available by author: $3.95 (plus applicable tax).   www.refractivethinker.com

Please send more FREE information:

❏ Speaking Engagements

❏ The Lentz Leadership Institute Educational Seminars

❏ Consulting

Join our Mailing List

Name: _____

Address: _____

City: _____ State: _____ Zip: _____

Telephone: _____ Email: _____

Sales tax: Please add 8.1% for shipping to NV addresses.

Shipping: *Please see website or contact us for exact shipping rates.*

The Lentz
Leadership
Institute LLC

Please send the following books:

☐ *The Refractive Thinker™: Volume I:*
An Anthology of Higher Learning

☐ *The Refractive Thinker™: Volume II:*
Research Methodology

☐ *The Refractive Thinker™: Volume III:*
Change Management

Paperback: $18.95 plus applicable tax and shipping.
E-books: $12.95 plus applicable tax.
Individual e-chapters available by author: $3.95 (plus applicable tax).   www.refractivethinker.com

Please send more FREE information:

☐ Speaking Engagements

☐ The Lentz Leadership Institute Educational Seminars

☐ Consulting

Join our Mailing List

Name: _____

Address: _____

City: _____ State: _____ Zip: _____

Telephone: _____ Email: _____

Sales tax: Please add 8.1% for shipping to NV addresses.

Shipping: *Please see website or contact us for exact shipping rates.*

The Lentz
Leadership
Institute LLC

Participation in
Future Volumes of
The Refractive Thinker™

Yes I would like to participate in:

❏ **Doctoral Volume**(s) for a specific university or your organization:

Name: _____

❏ **Graduate Volume**(s) MasterMinds for a specific university or your organization:

Name: _____

❏ **Specialized Volume**(s) Sorority, Business, or Themed:

Name: _____

Name: _____

Address: _____

City: _____ State: _____ Zip: _____

Telephone: _____ Email: _____

Please mail or fax form to:

The Lentz Leadership Institute LLC
c/o Dr. Cheryl Lentz
9065 Big Plantation Ave.
Las Vegas, NV 89143-5440   USA.
Fax: 877-298-5172
www.refractivethinker.com